A spiritual-cheer from my friend, Todd, to you, my dear reader:

"Jesus is the reason.

Come&Live! Live with Jesus, live on fire, live with the personal conviction that Jesus lives in you.

Be an ambassador of hope. I'm telling you to live and walk out your faith. You are to be like Jesus to people around you, you're an ambassador of hope.

It's *"Christ in you, the hope of glory."* You have the opportunity to destroy hell in people's lives because of the Christ who lives within you. God wants to use you, not just to get people to heaven one day, but it's about heaven getting into you now until you get there.

One day we'll leave this tent and we'll be with Jesus. But, right now, we get to live fully charged with the Holy Ghost inside us--destroying hell everywhere we go.

Everyday, everywhere we go, there are supernatural encounters just waiting to happen."

Todd White
Lifestyle Christianity
lifestylechristianity.com

D0062501

One Thousand Risks

Fighting Fear for an Awkward, Awesome Life with Jesus

by Chad Johnson / chadisliving.com

Published by

Everett Brave Books

827 Cammack Ct.

Nashville, TN. 37205

info@comeandlive.com

To contact the author about speaking at your event, please visit chadisliving.com

Publisher's Note: This is not a work of fiction. Names, characters, places, and incidents are not a product of the author's imagination. Locales and public names are, in some cases, purposely removed for the sake of honor and safety. Any resemblance to actual people, or to businesses, companies, events, institutions or locales, is completely intentional.

Editor-in-chief: Beth Johnson

Developmental editor: Darcie Clemen

Copy editor: Ken Darrow

Proofreader: Kendall Davis

Cover design & interior formatting: Mark Thomas / coverness.com

ISBN: 978-0-9994712-0-3

ONE
THOU
SND
RISKS

FIGHTING FEAR

FOR AN AWKWARD, AWESOME

LIFE WITH JESUS.

CHAD JOHNSON

Kind Words From Friends.

Brian "Head" Welch,

Co-founder / KoRn & *New York Times* best-selling author of *Save Me From Myself*, *Stronger* and *With My Eyes Wide Open*.
brianheadwelch. net

Chad Johnson is fearless because he sincerely sees humanity as family. In his new book, *One Thousand Risks*, Chad shares intense faith-encounters he's had with people simply by getting out of his comfort zone and approaching strangers as the Spirit leads him. This is a real and honest look at a normal guy who's learned to hear God's voice through trial and error. Chad has thrown fear and insecurity aside, allowing Jesus to use him in radical new ways. After reading *One Thousand Risks*. . . will you?

Ryan J. Downey,

Longtime Journalist / *Billboard, MTV, The Hollywood Reporter*
Artist Manager / Demon Hunter
ryanjdowney.com

Even for the more skeptical (and let's face it, cynical) among us, it's impossible not to feel inspired around Chad Johnson. His faith is something palpable in the air surrounding him, an almost tangible electricity that supercharges everyone he meets, from prominent rock stars to the families living in dire poverty around the world. Chad isn't wearing a costume of piousness. He's as real and relatable as they come, which makes his persistent joy and insistence on the gospel all the more powerful in real life terms. *One Thousand Risks* is a book about forsaking the world in pursuit of saving the world, one person at a time, with the absolute trust of a child in the guidance and faithfulness of our Creator.

Melody Joy Murray,
Founder & CEO / JOYN
joyn.com
Engaging, vibrant words point to Jesus' ability in granting us the real, true, messy, extravagant life. In a world dominated by comfort and caution, *One Thousand Risks* takes us powerfully into a different life perspective, one of abandonment and boldness. This book addresses what we all desperately need and never stop wanting: a life more abundant! These stories reveal a shared longing, a desire for more, inviting us toward deeper, wider faith. Chad's transparency, authenticity, and practical examples encourage me to exercise and use my faith—to continue taking risks and to live bold.

Matty Mullins,
Memphis May Fire
mattymullins.com
Packed full of breathtaking transparency and earnest truth, it was impossible to put this book down! *One Thousand Risks* is for anyone (Christian or not) who wants to look inside the life of a man genuinely desiring to see God move.

Aaron Weiss,
Singer & Storyteller
mewithoutyou.com
After many years of not seeing Chad he sent me a book called *Seeking*

Allah, Finding Jesus, and I thought "Allah is Jesus. " What the hell do I know? Later he sent me *One Thousand Risks*, so I read some, cried a bit, and sent along a few grammar tips. We might not believe all the same things but Chad's got quite an energy about him, I think our ancestors came off the same spaceship.

Ray Ortlund,

Lead Pastor / Immanuel Nashville Church
immanuelnashville.com
Jesus is not the chaplain to anyone's status quo life. He is like the cowboy riding into town on a Saturday night, shooting the place up. Chad Johnson gets that. He took the simple but radical step of opening his life up completely to Jesus. In *One Thousand Risks*, Chad shows you how you can do the same. You won't regret it.

Mina Whitlock

YWAM Kona / The Tribe
ywamkona.com
One Thousand Risks encourages me to deliver hope to the hopeless, and the lost to a Father who loves them more than I can fathom. Chad's story stirs me to see people find their identity as radical world-changers, regardless of age, nationality, gender or gifting. This book is calling you and me, all of us, to invest in restoring a hurting world by becoming who we were always meant to be.

Joel Richardson,

New York Times Best-selling author, speaker, filmmaker, missions catalyst.
joelstrumpet.com

One Thousand Risks is a great reminder that God rewards faith, is ever-present in times of struggle, and truly desires to continue working through us, even as He works in us. Any follower of Jesus who wants to develop a life of greater risk in God needs to read this book. Chad Johnson is fighting fear for a messy, extravagant life with Jesus. Now you can too.

Toby Morrell,

Co-Founder / BadChristian
badchristian.com

Chad is the most innocent, naive, generous, friendly criminal you could ever meet. This guy is just wild. In the same sentence, he's totally sold out to God and Christ, and yet also struggles with everything that everybody else does—almost like there's this attraction that he has to darkness and light waring inside of him. You don't feel more encouraged than when you're around Chad. There is a real spirituality to Chad that makes you believe. Chad makes you feel great even when you're saying the worst things about yourself.

Andy Byrd

YWAM / Circuit Riders / Fire & Fragrance Ministries
crmovement.com

It is amazing to watch how God is raising up so many unique voices with a passion for Christ-centered living and cultural reformation. Chad shares my heart to raise up a revival generation that lives in the confluence of a zealous love for God and a sincere love for others! May

Jesus work through *One Thousand Risks* to equip you for a life more extravagant than anything you could imagine.

Jennifer Case Cortez,

Contributor to *The Mom's Bible* and *Women on Life: A Call to Love the Unloved, Unborn, & Neglected*

jennifercasecortez.com

For a cautious, analytical, painfully self-conscious person like me, Chad Johnson's invitation to live a life of risk sounds like an Evite to a combat zone. *Thanks for thinking of me, Chad, but no.* Still, I've seen the Spirit of God move through Chad's prayers for others and in the life of my own family. Reading *One Thousand Risks* has been like having my own personal grace-filled, slightly-crazy risk coach nudging me to follow Jesus into places I've been too scared to go.

Seth Tower Hurd,

Relevant Magazine / Neighbors Again Podcast

I met Chad in 2007 to write a story about him for *Relevant Magazine*. It was like hopping into a car with an Old Testament prophet. Every time I've hung out with Chad, I've walked away inspired to live a more Christ-like, meaningful, beautiful life. Take the journey through this book, and you'll be changed too.

Rocky Braat,

Blood Brother

bloodbrotherfilm.com

Chad is a breath of fresh air to so many who have been disillusioned by Christians. His approachability, humility, and honesty are disarming. *One Thousand Risks* draws us back to the simple message that we are all dearly loved.

Josh Garrels,

Recording Artist, Musical Engineer, Label Owner

joshgarrels.com

It lights this little flame in me, which I think is probably Chad's deal. He goes somewhere and starts a fire in that place and shows people that more is possible. Healing has not necessarily been a known path for me. In my mind, I've known it's possible, that Jesus is all powerful, but I hadn't personally seen or taken part in healing very often. Maybe a handful of times in the ten years since I've been a believer. So, to have God's power placed back on the radar with Chad, and then inviting me into it. . . there's energy, mental and spiritual energy, that's given. I've seen the Lord work in real time to heal my buddy's ear by degrees, what even turned into a beautiful time.

Matt Carter,

Co-Founder / BadChristian

badchristian.com

Chad takes it to another level. He invests in people as a mentor, a guide, and a spiritual leader, even becoming vulnerable to the point where it could threaten his own personal success. Chad is the most legendary A&R guy in the history of Tooth and Nail Records. Here's some simple, fun, math: by my count, Chad worked with around 50 bands, most bands having four or five people, so just like that we're talking 200-250 people that Chad was the A&R guy for. Chad was their mentor, their brother, even their father-figure perhaps, somebody that prayed for them, somebody that invested in them deeply, and authentically. Here's the crazy thing about that; these aren't just 250 people, these are 250 public figures that sold, combined, near ten million records. So, his influence is almost unimaginable, incalculable at least.

My favorite part about Chad's success is that he achieved it in large part due to his quirky personality and that people found him to be trustworthy, explaining to them directly just how untrustworthy he was by exposing and owning his flaws. Chad is authentic, transparent and real. In an era where people are less that—authentic, transparent and real—especially in the music business, Chad cut through. He's influenced other people, myself included, to do the same.

Jooly Philip,

English Professor & Anti-Trafficking Advocate

bombayteenchallenge.com

For as long as I have known Chad, I have perceived him to be someone who challenges and encourages others (and himself) to make Christ relevant in a hurt and broken world. *One Thousand Risks* reflects Chad's heart to take up the challenge of boldly and lovingly engaging people from all walks of life, often speaking to them about the immediate needs in their lives, and ultimately pointing them to a Savior who is *for* them.

Ben Crist,

Worship Leader & Recording Artist / The Glorious Unseen

Chad has been a personal friend and mentor to me for over ten years now. His passion for Jesus and relentless pursuit of the presence of God is contagious! He always stirs me and challenges me to pursue God with total abandon. Read *One Thousand Risks* and find yourself inspired.

Aaron Lunsford,

Author of *Backstage: How I Almost Got Rich Playing Drums in a Christian Hardcore Band*

aaronlunsford.com

Chad was my A&R guy. He's pretty intense and always operating on that full-speed level; super inspired, very excited, making you feel like everything's going to be OK and your band is going to do great. He went from not just being our advocate at the label when our van broke down, but he'd also say, "Hey, let me pray with you and make sure you're not going to kill yourself while you're on the road."

Jake Luhrs,

Singer, August Burns Red / Founder, Heart Support & More Weight

heartsupport.com

We played Cornerstone Festival, and I remember Chad was watching a band called Life In Your Way when he noticed me side-stage and approached me saying, "Hey man, I just want you to know I see Jesus all over you." And, Chad, at Cornerstone, was just praying for people and it was inspiring to me. Then when he said what he did to me, it was really encouraging. I remember after the Life In Your Way show, Underoath was headlining. So I ran over to the main stage to watch them play and noticed a girl who had somehow been injured, she was laying in an ambulance. I had never prayed for anybody in my entire life, but watching Chad pray for people and then hearing him tell me that he saw Jesus all over me, I laid my hands on the hood of the ambulance and I prayed for that girl. That was my first real shot at letting the Holy Spirit in, really bringing my faith to a different level.

TD & Veronica Benton,

Traveling Theatrical Performers / White Collar Sideshow
whitecollarsideshow.com

Jesus never promises a life of safety or security, but He does offer a life of abundance. Chad is one of the crazy-brave who, through seeking Jesus, has been able to experience that abundant life. During every encounter with Chad, we find ourselves challenged, encouraged and inspired. He will pause a phone conversation to pray with the barista at a coffee shop or stop and pray with an unsuspecting person on the way back to the car after a meal. Each time, we step back and see Jesus. We see Jesus working through Chad's obedience, but we also see Jesus in the person receiving prayer. Chad has worked through his fears to take risks for the kingdom. *One Thousand Risks* is not about Chad taking risks, *One Thousand Risks* is about bringing heaven to earth.

Wesley Zinn,

Senior Associate Pastor / Wellspring Church
wellspring. net

Inspiring. Challenging. Even convicting at times. Chad's personal testimony of living faith through the doorway of risk should stir us all. I appreciate his humility. Through his honesty and vulnerability we see that each of us can radically love those around us, making room for God's power and presence to transform lives. Read this book with an open mind and an open heart.

Daniel Norris,

Communications Coordinator / Youth With A Mission

danielnorris.com

In the midst of our hyper-busy lives, *One Thousand Risks* will interrupt you in the best way possible. Not only will it challenge your faith, but it will do so in a way where faith always feels attainable. From the first time I met Chad, to every moment spent in between, it was clear that he was a man who walked what he taught. This book encompasses a "do-first-then-teach" mentality in such a pure and humble way. Whether you are new to the faith, or in full-time ministry, I hope you are willing to let *One Thousand Risks* lead you into a new normal.

Mark W. Castrogiovanni

Founder & Senior Pastor / The Tabernacle

tabernacleonline.com

Fearless honesty, wit, and transparency of real-life experiences make *One Thousand Risks* a must read. Most of us live in the theater seats of life, when we were created to lead the adventure. The very thing that is begging for life to be full is risk. Chad will encourage you to live a bold, hopeful life, "the one God created you for." This book will be alongside some of the great champions of the faith in our church bookstore and in my personal library. Love it!

Scott Johnson,

Lead Pastor / The Pointe Fellowship

thepointeministry. org

My brother takes his readers on a treacherous, outrageous, and life-changing journey into the world of surrendering all to Jesus Christ. The stories throughout *One Thousand Risks* are as real, raw and inspiring as they come. Chad's tenacity and unrelenting pursuit of obedience to Jesus have greatly influenced my life.

James Allen,

Entrepreneurial Leader & Communications Strategist / Life In Your Way

There isn't a story in this book that I haven't either witnessed firsthand; been present with a group who witnessed it firsthand; or heard from Chad within days of its occurrence. Few people have walked as closely with Chad through the period from which the stories in *One Thousand Risks* took place. Our friendship has given me a window into the greatest gifts that Chad possesses as well as his greatest weaknesses. Through it all, I've seen something simple and refreshing: an ordinary man in need of grace, believing in an extraordinary God.

The transparency with which Chad lives his life, the same spirit in which this book is written, will undoubtedly attract praise and criticism alike. One thing is certain: Chad's authenticity is real. Spend more than an hour with Chad anywhere and I guarantee you'll have one of the most awkward (and sometimes awesome) experiences of your life. So it is with this book!

Craig Gross,

Author & Founder

XXXchurch.com

Jesus never played it safe, but somehow we live in a world filled with Christians building more hospitals for healthy people than ever before. In *One Thousand Risks*, Chad helps us realize who Jesus was and encourages us to live like Him.

Nathan Mallon,

Technical Advisor / Dave Ramsey

daveramsey.com

Chad's made a significant impact on my life by provoking my desire to value Jesus and other people more than my desire to feel comfortable, important or in control. Although obedience may look different for each of us, *One Thousand Risks* will inspire you to overcome whatever obstacles are preventing you from thriving in *the messy, extravagant new.*

Chad Pearson,

Chief Operating Officer / Reach Records

reachrecords.com

As the other "Chad" in the industry, I have always admired Chad for having the strength to follow Jesus in walking away from the music business. Many questioned why in the hell he was doing this, but if you were to have a conversation with Chad you'd quickly find your answer.

Chad's passion for Christ and for people to know Him is contagiously evident in reading *One Thousand Risks*. As a fellow missionary kid and music industry veteran, *One Thousand Risks* hits closer to home then I would like to admit. I'm ready to take my first risk of one thousand.

Corey Pigg,

Podcast Producer / The Liturgists & The Bible for Normal People, Host / Failed Missionary

failedmissionary.com

Chad and I have been close friends for many years. He was the first mentor in ministry who taught me to love others well. While our journey as "missionaries" has placed us on opposite ends of the faith spectrum, our dedication to loving others has remained unscathed. *One Thousand Risks* is everything I know Chad to be - vivid, honest, awkward. I loved reading and reliving memories. Chad's love for others is radical, his personality is whimsical, and I trust you will enjoy spending this time with him.

Sean Feucht,

Bethel Music Artist & Founder / Burn 24-7

seanfeucht.com

I've been watching God move across the nations, having traveled well over 3 million miles in the last 12 years, where I'm constantly being reminded of Habakkuk 1:5; *"Look among the nations, and see; wonder and be astounded. For I am doing a work in your days that you would not believe if told."* The wild tales that Chad shares in *One Thousand Risks* point to the reality of Jesus performing a work in our day that is truly astounding. My prayer is that One Thousand Risks stirs your heart to burn with renewed faith, vision, and a sacrificial pursuit after the presence of God.

Ravi Kandal,

Conference Speaker & Co-Founder / Kingdom Foundations

kingdomfoundations.org

Have you ever wondered; "there must be more in following Christ?" Have you had an unexplainable hunger for God, sensing a deeper realm in Him, only to feel that it's entirely out of reach? Then *One Thousand Risks* is for you. Chad's stories will open your eyes to the possibilities God has made available to every believer. I expect this book to inspire you with insights from the God-process which has changed Chad's approach to life. God is inviting us all to embark on the journey where hearing, and responding to His voice, become a lifestyle of obedience. Expect to be taken into a realm of supernatural encounters that only God's grace could orchestrate. This book--like it's author--is authentic, practical, and compelling. Chad is a good friend, a champion, my brother-in-law, and one of my heroes in the faith. His life challenges me by the way he chases courage in the face of fear and impossibilities. Join him in watching your impossibilities turned God-possibilities.

Jodi Pierce,

Co-Founder / Steiger International

steiger.org

I am always looking for people who push me to live out the supernatural, miraculous life described in the Book of Acts. Chad Johnson is one of those people. *One Thousand Risks* is full of astounding, personal stories that will inspire you to change your life; to no longer be satisfied with following God in an ordinary, powerless way. This book will teach you how to risk a life of surrender to God, leading you to one adventure after another, for the rest of your life.

Tommy Green,

Founder / The REV Gatherings & Vocalist / Sleeping Giant

theREVGatherings.com

It's been my unique privilege to have been present with Chad during some of the moments where the Holy Spirit was awakening him most. We have risked together from concerts in Oklahoma to the streets of Bogotá, watching in wonder as Jesus answered our shaky, trembling prayers of faith. I remember being shocked when I asked Chad how long he had been operating in signs and wonders. His response was child-like and telling; "What are signs and wonders?" Though God was already using Chad to advance His kingdom on earth, he hadn't heard of *When Heaven Invades Earth*, studied theology, or experienced a single year of ministry training. What Chad had was courage, vulnerability, and hunger. *One Thousand Risks* is the quintessential guide for anyone who desires to grow their Holy Spirit dependency toward world-changing potential.

Mattie Montgomery,

Founder / AwakeningEvangelism & Vocalist / For Today
mattiemongtomery.com

I've been honored to know Chad Johnson for many years. And in all the various moments and capacities in which we have worked together, I have known him to be one thing above and before all else; a man fully committed to following the gentle tug of God on his heart. In One Thousand Risks, Chad invites us to explore the awesome and awkward moments that have come out of his "yes" to God. He writes with brave humility and ardent simplicity. Wherever you find yourself, Chad's story of radical, reckless obedience to the call of God will challenge you to pursue the impossible. Risk everything for the sake of love.

Shaun Tabatt,

Host of The Shaun Tabatt Show

This book will challenge you to venture outside the walls of the church and boldly bring the love of Jesus to each person God puts in your path.

Dedicated to Beth, Sydney, and David. You remind me daily of what grace looks like.

There's only one God, ma'am, and I'm pretty sure he doesn't dress like that.
  - Captain America

Table of Contents.

Foreword.

I became a disciple of Jesus when I was a teenager, but it wasn't until a decade later that I witnessed a miraculous and instantaneous healing. Somewhere in the middle, I met Chad Johnson. He was an icon of independent music amongst those in the know—the director of A&R at what was one of the biggest independent record labels in the world. From DIY darlings to punk rock royalty, Chad seemed to fit right in at Tooth & Nail Records. After all, he'd paid his dues with his own little (failed) label, and every hardworking band knew his story. I won't bore you with the details, but in 2003, I shook Chad's hand for the first time, and about a year later he signed my band to his record label. During the 14 years that followed, at least two incredible things happened: Chad and I stuck with our life's work of apprenticing Jesus (to varying degrees of success and failure, of course), and well, we're still friends.

It would be a stretch of the truth to insist that I have always wanted one thing out of my life's work, but it stretches the truth less to say that I *wanted* to want one thing out of my life's work. What I've *wanted* to want was to be with Jesus, become like Jesus, and do what Jesus did. I have come to believe an incredible story of a first-century Jewish Rabbi in the ancient Near East who preached the coming of God's kingdom through word and deed. The story of God himself stepping down into the world, to conquer death by—of all things—dying. And that somehow, in light of this beautiful, mesmerizing and mysterious story there is an entirely new way to be human, and an entirely new reality breaking into the old one of death and dying. When someone becomes an apprentice of Jesus, their story ebbs and flows. There are times when practicing the way of Jesus comes wonderfully easy and times when it is like leaning your weight against a storm. Like marriage, you grow, and shift, and change, and yet choose to love and live and press on. All the while, you are becoming someone else. In theology, we call this *spiritual formation*—it happens gradually over time, but occasionally takes radical leaps forward. One such change in my apprenticeship to Jesus happened in Nashville when I asked Chad why he had begun to pray for miraculous healing, even over strangers. Moments later, I witnessed one such miracle myself.

In my years of travel, I have been privy to a world in desperate need of God's redemptive power. I've seen a people oppressed by selfishness, greed, addiction, listlessness, anxiety, depression, despair... I've seen a church co-opted by the American dream and a generation taught to settle for the feeble, plastic freedom of more stuff, more distraction, more safety, more comfort. I've concluded, time and time again, that the world does indeed need Jesus and that Jesus is indeed at work in the world.

But after that evening praying with Chad, I began to see new things.

I saw a middle-aged woman weep in front of a crowd of young people because God had healed her long pain-ridden feet. I saw a young man baffled by the fact that even though he did not believe God could or would heal his neck of chronic pain, God did it anyway. A young woman in Florida bawled in front of us as she confessed that it was on that night she first believed that God truly loved her. A group of perfect strangers in New York huddled around one another, joining hands and crying out to God on behalf of a wayward family member none of us knew. I have seen eyes and ears opened to see and hear. I've seen tumors vanish, terminal illness beaten back, demonic oppression brought to an end. I've seen relationships mended, marriages restored, hope made plain to the hopeless.

It is my job to study the Scriptures. Most days of the week I read theologians and scholars and ancient manuscripts—pouring over the Bible in an ongoing effort to unravel its endless layers. On paper, theology is captivating; it stirs the heart and mind and seizes the imagination. In person, theology is devastating; it shocks a man to his very core to see with his own eyes, and feel in his very bones, the truth that prayer changes reality and that Jesus, God of the universe, is moving in the world today.

One Thousand Risks is about that very thing. In these pages ahead, Chad asks two questions I believe to be among the most pressing any human being might consider: Who is Jesus, and what if the things He said and did were actually true?

Chad is—like most people who long to become like Jesus—not one for pretense. It's just as well, because I realize my friend is imperfect. Be that as it may, I am grateful to have learned from him, and I suspect I will continue to do so. For a guy who studies theology for a living, Chad is a much-needed curveball—the fellow who suggests: Yes, that *is* true, so then what do *we do* about it?

Joshua S. Porter
September 16, 2017
joshdies.com

A Letter to My Reader Who Does Not Follow Jesus.

For starters, there are two things I would like your heart to hear from mine:

First, I love that you're here regardless of what you do or don't believe about Jesus. And, secondly, I apologize to you for any time you may have been hurt, rejected, embarrassed, or mistreated by me (or anyone else claiming to follow Jesus). Christians may be imperfect, but you deserve honor, respect, and love from all of us, way above any excuse we might make for our mistakes.

It's essential for you to know that, even though I was once similarly where you are, I've written this book primarily for followers of Jesus. You might want to read it merely out of curiosity, and I applaud the notion. Some of the language and ideas may bewilder you as I'm communicating mostly as an evangelist to Evangelicals.

Romans 3:23 (a New Testament Bible book written by the Apostle Paul) says, *"for all have sinned and fall short of the glory of God."* If you've never heard what the Spirit of God has written through broken people, be encouraged by the great company you're in. All our first, middle, and last names were once Sinner. Download *Bible (the app)* to your phone and start reading wherever you want. *The Book of Acts* is a great starting point. Jesus' response to you is past and present. Even more so, future.

There's no pressured bait and switch scam driving my sinister inspiration here. I've placed a heartfelt spiritual invitation for you at the end of this letter, but I'm telling you upfront with nothing to hide because I value you and your time. Jesus isn't the David Blaine of soul magic; He honors too much to pull slick-looking tricks on you.

My adventurous calling of a message to you is of utter importance—I do believe that.

If you choose to read no further, I will understand and applaud you all the same. One reason why the name "Jesus" is on the cover is that I didn't want you to mistake the voice of my book for coming from any direction but a straight-ahead Christian one.

When Jesus saved me, I was drug-addicted, girl-crazed, an all-paths-lead-to-god eighteen-year-old living wild in South America. While on the verge of being arrested for the distribution of narcotics, I asked my best friend at the time (now my beautiful wife of twenty + years) what I should do.

Though not the response I wanted to hear, her answer was simple: "Ask Jesus for help."

That very night, January 10th, 1992, I dropped to my knees and prayed something like:

Jesus, I don't even know if You're real. I don't know if You are who people or the Bible say You are. But, if You are real, would You please show Yourself? I need help. And if You're out there wanting in here, I'll take Your help. Please forgive my sins and my failures. Help me. Amen.

I wouldn't have called it a faith-filled prayer, because at that time I didn't have faith in Jesus. But I was sincere. I was also in trouble, and a trusted friend told me Jesus could help. That was enough potential reward for the risk.

There is a *serious* difference between Jesus and religion. Every religion, including Christianity when it becomes *works* oriented—meaning we *earn* approval with God based on what we do—is rooted in self-motivation, willpower, or the idea that we must reach God on our own. Jesus is *not* religion. He is not a political party or an ideal. He's not a polite statue hanging dead on a cross. He's a person, and He is more alive than any of us know. He lives in hearts who invite Him in. He was a revolutionary Person two thousand years ago, and He is still revolutionizing people now. Your life will never be full *or* fulfilled until Jesus is the One directing you.

Living for Jesus is stupid radical and yet fully worth your consideration. Why not leave behind what you were never meant for in exchange of a spiritual enterprise that is not safe, often messy, but extravagant on levels incalculable? You're not here by accident. What are the odds of all the billions of people in the world—and you and I living in spaces far removed from each other—that we would find ourselves right here?

Like any of us, what do you *really* stand to lose? If I'm a liar—simply another semi-gifted snake-oil salesman—you have nothing to fear. Why not invite Jesus to help you, to live inside you, and to take charge of your destiny? If He isn't real, you'll forget the prayer, and at some point laugh at the idea, 'random Christian writer guy' actually convinced you to pray.

If Jesus is real, you have all His presence to gain, not to mention the best of best friends. Jesus is my friend. We're in relationship, abiding together. I want to be more like Him because He's perfect and loves unlike anyone I've met. He treats everyone as they were meant to be treated. He loves unconditionally.

Jesus isn't threatening Hell so you'll embrace Him, he's embracing you so you'll threaten Hell.

Give Him your life. Give Him your all. Even now. I'm thirty thousand feet above the Atlantic Ocean, tears are filling my eyes, and I'm self-consciously hoping my neighbor doesn't notice. Jesus cries with you every time you've been hurt, are hurting, or hurt someone else. He is the long-awaited Messiah, Savior of the world, the only true path to God and life fully realized. He's not just a prophet or a moral example. Even more than respect, He wants your life. Hand Him the keys. Surrender.

If you don't have a clue who Jesus is, ask Him to reveal Himself. If He's real, how could He not? Ask Him to show you His perspective, to share His life with you. Give Him whatever you have. He will gladly trade your *unremarkable old* for all His abundant fullness. I promise no genuine "Jesus save me!" prayer will go unheard. It doesn't matter whether you come with arms open or bearing arms. Just come.

Change may occur instantaneously for you, something I've seen happen many times. Or change may develop more like my process: Jesus washing you clean day by day, seemingly slow and uneventful, at first. What I can tell you is that I've been following Jesus for over twenty-five years and I'm still not very good at it. But my life is full and all kinds of *messy extravagant.* Yes, it's sometimes extremely difficult—Jesus promised hardships, misunderstandings, and persecutions for believing in Him.

If your heart is rapidly beating in your chest right now, you sense a nervous energy, an aura/vibe, or simply think, Oh, what the hell do I have to lose? Well, true, you do have Hell to lose. Who wants Hell anyway? We've already lived there too often. We weren't meant to pray a prayer that zaps us from the challenges of this life straight into eternal bliss. Our calling is to leave *the unremarkable old* for *the messy, extravagant new.* With God's help, all the time, everywhere. Life is abundant. Death is gain. Pray with me right now:

Jesus, I honestly have no clue if You're real. I don't even know how in the world I made it to this prayer. But, I really don't have much to lose. So, if You are real, please show me. I invite You to come and live inside my heart and make my life what You want it to be: fear free. I give You all my sins, my mistakes, my pain, my deep-rooted issues; every problem. Please take them and replace them with everything that would bring You glory and fame. I bring you even the stuff I'm most afraid to give up. Here I am, a sinner. But, if You are King of the Universe, I'd like You to make me a saint. I welcome this fruit of Your Spirit to speak louder than anything else in my life: love, joy, peace, patience, kindness, gentleness, faithfulness, goodness, self-control. I invite the Holy Spirit to help me. Holy Spirit, if You are real, and if Jesus is real, here's my life. Show me the goodness of the Father. Baptize me with Heavenly power. Amen.

Amazing! Even if you didn't pray this prayer because you already are following Jesus (and wondered what I might say to someone who isn't following Him yet) or because you're just not ready, I think God placed me here on Earth just to encourage you, to remind you of your value and your potential. I celebrate your courage in doing what I likely never would have: your reading of this letter proves risk-taking on a level I aspire to reach.

Thank you for being brave enough to bear even temporarily with a faith-optimist like me. If you did pray this prayer, please contact me. My email address is chad@comeandlive.com. I'd love to pray for you and serve you every way I can on this thrill of a journey ahead.

If you did just invite Jesus in, I pray you realize that you're now reading as a freshly adopted member of the family. Welcome. We're better for having you with us!

Chad Johnson

Preface: The Risk Preceding One Thousand.

Nine years ago I had what you might call an epiphany, but what I would consider a spiritual awakening. Back then I was positioned in a thriving music career where I was responsible for finding, signing and developing bands, what is known in the industry as A&R (Artists & Repertoire) work. Even though I loved music, I never studied music or business, have no rhythm, am unable to carry a tune, and can't play a single instrument. I felt an earnest appreciation to be a part of a team that was pioneering careers for wildly talented artists. My spiritual epiphany, to combine what we both could call it, was the awareness that being a privileged music guy wasn't the path meant for my life.

The problem was, I couldn't stop dreaming of something different. Still, I was afraid that leaving would result in career suicide. I had a young family depending entirely on my income. I didn't have total clarity as to what I would do once I exited the music industry, and had no back-up plan for when everything fell apart. I was even more fearful, though, that if I didn't follow my heart, I would forever regret the unknown of what could, or would, have been. As I clambered for direction or any kind of confirmation that I hadn't just gone spiritually insane, the Holy Spirit peacefully and unexpectedly gave me four simple, bold instructions:

1. Make your life all about Jesus
2. Stop worrying about money
3. Make disciples of artists and others

4. Give yourself away

My true calling came at the peak of my music industry success—an unexpected, undeserved twelve-year career generously affixing my name to an album or two. With my wife's nervous blessing, I abruptly left the conventional music world, one part impassioned and three parts foolish.

I cashed out my 401(k), gold plaques, the record collection, and began living an adventure that has led me, reluctantly, to every continent on the planet with *Come&Live!*, a nonprofit community several friends and I started in response to those four instructions which the Spirit had given me.

Not following Jesus and what Jesus was saying to my heart, would have been the safest option available to me. No one was asking me, much less telling me, to leave the music industry. Years later, I'm fairly sure that I would have in due course failed because my heart had lost all the passion it once had for the business of music. It's hard to stay alive very long without passion.

Maybe I could have tried harder to re-engage, or maybe I could have given the whole thing another shot. As fathers, providing for our families is a huge responsibility that we can't ever ignore. Truth be told, I prayerfully contemplated my music industry dismissal for nearly three years before eventually putting in my notice. If I were given a "do-over" I would have exited very differently, especially in terms of how quickly I distanced myself from artists and friends I had the honor of growing up with.

The temptation to avoid risk would have been safe, but I would have only been a facade. Ultimately, I would have missed a life layered with thousands of risks.

You were meant to live and model risk, but you were never meant to grow alone. You've been invited into a great story of daring significance, where realizing how much potential you've been carrying, is only the beginning. If I can help convince you that a life of risk is the right move, even when it's hard to hear, and still harder to apply, we'll both be tuned to the sound of a world shifting.

One Thousand Risks was written for you, my Christian brother or sister, regardless of where you *feel* you are, whether living closer to Jesus than ever or considering why further does *seem* forever. For you, dreamer of revival so huge *the unremarkable old* couldn't possibly contain you. And for you, spiritually starved and barely alive, wondering if faith abandoned would prove the more excellent way. In the short term, it might appear so. But that's not nearly as dangerous or exhilarating as your prodigal resurrection.

My aim is to point you to a fresh, authentic experience *with* the God who loves you even when you *think* you (or God) are as unlovable as ever. I haven't written from the angle of "author has life all figured out." Instead, I'm writing from the perspective of an unlikely word-scribbler, am uniting hands with brothers, sisters—future brothers and sisters—calling you deeper into an ancient and honest narrative, shouting loud encouragement as we go and grow together.

This book is a personal, humble letter inviting you where I never thought I could go, teaching you where I was once far too reluctant, for fear I wasn't brave enough. My commitment is in serving you, even if that means stretching way beyond where either of us feels comfortable, or sharing my heart with restless conviction, despite the possibility our beliefs may presently land us worlds apart.

Equipping you for a life of risk is why I write.

God, here I am. Please send me. My life is Yours. I'd rather give it away than selfishly hold back, though the temptation to make a habit out of holding back still lurks.

1. An Introduction.

The smallest deed is better than the greatest intention.
- John Burroughs

Jesus said to him, "Get up, take up your bed, and walk." And at once the man was healed, and he took up his bed and walked.
- John 5:8&9.

Have you ever sensed that you were being set up for something grand? Something way bigger than you could possibly pull off on your own?

I found myself standing in the Bronx after an all-night prayer vigil when my attention was suddenly drawn, directed even, to a man seated in a wheelchair. A year prior, Mike had been in the backseat of a taxi when a large delivery truck smashed into the cab, crushing his legs from the knees down. Doctors had not anticipated salvaging his legs. Surgery was surprisingly successful, although Mike hadn't been able to use his legs since. Over the past year, his legs had gone completely numb with no feeling whatsoever—other than extreme pain. I thanked Mike for sharing a piece of his story, and asked if my friend and I could pray over his legs. As he nodded in agreement, we began praying short prayers commanding his legs to be made whole again, something along these lines: *Pain leave. Muscles, bones, tendons: be strengthened. Legs work and operate the way you were made to.*

Mike responded to my question on what he was feeling, "You know, it's funny. It's almost like someone shot electricity down my kneecaps into my legs." I asked if he normally felt these "shooting shocks" down his legs. Never in his life had he felt anything like them. We prayed a little while longer, and I again asked Mike what he was feeling. "Well, it's like all the numbness that was there is just gone. And there's only a little pain I feel in my left ankle." We commanded pain to leave his left ankle. I asked Mike to try putting pressure on his legs. He did so while keeping all his weight on his arms. He sat heavily back in the chair, looked up at us, and then broke out with a smile, "That actually felt really good."

We moved Mike to a more level area and asked if we could lock arms on either side to try holding him up. Kindly, he agreed. Keep in mind; we had just met Mike. He didn't know us from any other stranger and yet was willing to trust us like brothers. There we stood, arms locked, for nearly ten minutes. Mike even took a few baby steps without any directive from either of us. The thought came to my head (though in the immediate I had no idea why) insisting that Mike should stop looking at his legs, which seemed to be his natural response. To look up and around instead. He complied, marveling, "The perspective from up here is so nice, everything has a certain glow to it." I took my arm out from under his and within a few minutes motioned for my friend to do the same. There Mike was—standing in the Bronx—completely unassisted with 100% of his weight on previously crushed legs. I quietly wept, foolishly pretending I wasn't as shocked as he was. Mike then surprised us by saying he was going to walk. "My legs feel so good and so strong, I'm just going to go for it." I quickly questioned his enthusiasm, "Do you want us to hold your hands or stand closer by you?" He was confident, "No, I'm fine." He then took about eight steps, completely unassisted, turned around, and walked back to his chair. He did this on three different occasions, once while pushing his chair around. We asked how he felt. His only "issue" was realizing the soreness in his legs from all the walking/standing energy he had just exerted.

"I could walk a thousand miles, but my muscles need to catch up with my heart."

For most of my Christian life, I have felt exactly the same way that Mike described the tension between his heart and legs. My heart has desired to walk a thousand miles closer to loving God and loving neighbors. Though my faith muscles weren't smashed by a delivery truck, they seem to have painfully atrophied all the same—resulting in a consistent struggle to catch up.

One thousand risks interrupted everything I thought I knew about loving God and neighbors. I was hungry to experience more of God in my routine, daily existence when Jesus challenged me to the greatest level of Holy Spirit obedience since the day I unenthusiastically challenged Him to save my soul. The kind of stepping out of my way for others, like Mike from the Bronx, a little more as the God of the universe does. Stopping for. Giving to. Praying and sharing with. Hearing from. Laughing together. Embracing.

Fast forward a year after my experience in the Bronx, and I was sipping coffee across the table from my wife, Beth. It was December 31, 2012, and I possessed no clearer directive from Jesus for a New Year's resolution than silence rattling my skull. The only thought slightly stirring was that of possibly attempting to pray for every sick and hurting person I came across. I mentioned this risky, just-pray-for-them-all, stepping and stumbling idea to Beth. Typical to her style, she immediately offered a more profound suggestion: "What about all the people who aren't obviously hurting? Why not just make a goal instead to take one thousand risks?"

Inspiration hummed, echoed, and chorused through my veins. I slowly sounded it out: One. Thousand. Risks. The "Aha!" moment of a bold plan had been birthed. Daily risks motivated by love, bound not by days, months or even years, followed by a short synopsis of how the experience went—good or bad. What if I shared it all? What if you share it all? Encouraging stories, discouraging tales, and, Lord-willing, the great endgame result of saints and sinners better equipped to live in the new land of *messy extravagance.* Beth's dare instantly spiraled my thoughts into a fidgety excitement toward one thousand individual risks with no deadline in sight.

Then the not-so-inspiring concern crossed my mind, "Is risk-taking even Biblical?"

According to the English Standard Version of the Bible, the word "risk" or "risked" is *only* listed three times in all of the New Testament: *"1. . . . men who have risked their lives for the name of our Lord Jesus Christ. 2. . . . who risked their necks for my life. . . 3. . . . risking his life to complete what was lacking in your service to me."*[1] All three instances place the context in risking *lives, necks,* and *life* for the sake of others knowing Jesus. Though the word "risk" barely appears in the New Testament, Hebrews chapter 11 proves the concept of risk is littered throughout the whole Bible as the appropriate response to faith.

The action *to* risk always follows a conviction *from* faith. Think of the greatest risk you've ever taken in life. Where were you? What was it? And would you have taken that risk without confidence—even if minimally present? Would I have asked Beth to marry me had I known she loved someone else? Would I have left my music industry job just to experiment with homelessness? Would you have picked up this book without even a little hope that your life could be different? I'm nowhere near funny enough to win your heart or clever enough to win your head. The best bet I have for "convincing" you is the Holy Spirit because He keeps convincing me. Faith is a seed planted. Risk is faith sprouting.

---

1 Acts 15:25&26, Romans 16:3&4, Philippians 2:29&30, respectively

Jesus, in an instant, through Beth, challenged me way further down into messy extravagance. He does have a way of speaking through those closest to us. Beth had been hugely inspired by Canadian-farmer-wife-turned-award-winning-author, Ann Voskamp, who wrote the *New York Times* bestseller *One Thousand Gifts*. In short, Ann's idea was listing those things daily she was grateful for with the goal of collecting a thousand unique "gifts." As a result, God used Ann to inspire a lifestyle of gratitude amongst countless others living too often in the *unremarkable old*. Her counting began, at least as far as I know, with a blog—aholyexperience.com—and grew into a global "giving thanks" movement of the more messy, extravagant kind. Ann has no idea how much her story has rerouted mine, just as I am clueless on how much my story is empowering yours, or as you don't yet realize how your story is igniting someone else. It only takes a spark.

Will you pause and consider the idea of stepping *consistently* out of your way—gradually learning to notice others as the King of the Universe notices them? What if you asked God for grace to take even one *daily* risk? Maybe a short prayer over someone struggling? Sharing a story with an unexpected somebody. Laughing with he or she who is rarely laughed with. Giving a sliver of your heart, hopefully even a little slice of His, in the process.

One thousand risks. Or however many you want. Even one single risk to love a neighbor is a bold step, but don't put a timeline on these risks. Each risk is stretching you and I beyond fear, safety and ourselves. Learning to discern God's heart—translated by the Spirit's help—for one hugely-loved-by-Jesus person at a time. Leaving *the unremarkable old* for a *messy, extravagant new*.

One thousand risks took me 740 days, averaging around one risk a day—except when I took 40 risks on my 40th birthday for the sheer fun of only turning 40 once. I encountered the heart of God one person after the next, making notes on my phone after the risk to help me keep track of each experience. Along the way, I discerned markedly more about myself, God, and others. I witnessed more miracles in two years than in all my previous 38 years combined. Most of all, I learned that fighting fear is a required lesson for obtaining an awkward, awesome life with Jesus. My goal was to see my own Jesus-journey challenged. Possibly even inspiring you in the process is icing on the cake. Jesus left ninety-nine sheep in relative safety to pursue one which was lost. My desire was, and still is, growth in His footsteps.

Thinking ahead for you, I foresee seven likely scenarios.

1. Times of rejection, a reaction Jesus promised would find you.
2. It is entirely possible you might be misunderstood.
3. Instances where words won't come out the way you mean them to, either because you are nervous, anxious or not able to process encouraging thoughts quickly enough.
4. Opportunities to drop risk at the first *sight* or *feeling* of impossibility, running instead toward all too familiar *unremarkable old* comfort.
5. Hopeful expectation stirring you.
6. Learning to love others as Jesus loved. And loves. Seeing others the way they were intended to be seen.
7. Your dependency on the Spirit's leading will increase. Sizably.

Despite the downside, I promise you a world will open that is so full and so rich—a well worth treasuring—like living water to those dying from thirst. Francis Chan, a radical risk-taker who I respect immensely, says it like this: "I'm not asking you to do something you're going to hate. Yeah, there will be times when it's rough and whatever else. But, I'm asking you to actually do something where at the end of your life, you'll have a fulfillment that says, 'I am stoked for all eternity because of what

I did on that little planet. ""[2]

I'm inviting you to live on risk. *"The wicked flee when no one pursues but the righteous are bold as a lion."* (Proverbs 28:1). Following Christ is the most dangerous decision you have—or will—ever make. If no one told you before you began following Jesus this jungle was wild, I am deeply sorry. You must feel caught entirely off guard already, by all my outlandish suggestions.

The first thought to cross my mind, possibly crossing yours, is whether I could, or would, actually learn to care for others in ways more closely relating to Jesus. I had never taken anything like this on. Ever. Naturally, I was afraid and greatly unsure of whether I was disciplined and courageous enough to take on a dare as audacious as this. If you can relate, be encouraged to know you're far from alone. God doesn't despise even our smallest of beginnings.

My ambition isn't to give you an exhaustive list of one thousand great risks gone one thousand great ways. I'm aiming at inspiring you to practice the lost art of listening to God and noticing neighbors. In painting authentic, sometimes flawed pictures; equipping *the messy, extravagant you* to go and grow despite weakness trying to stop or reverse your potential. The apostle Paul is a rebellious reminder that improbability serves as the kind of substance heavenly grace sails through. Jesus cares (regardless of how you currently care for Him). He is there when you are weak and present when you are strong. He is here. Even when we don't believe He is.

I've made many mistakes in the last year alone, not to mention my whole life. Still, our *unremarkable old* matters. Without it, there is no *messy, extravagant new* worth stepping into. Here's what I mean by these two phrases (*the unremarkable old* and *messy, extravagant new)* that I

---

2 https://www. youtube.com/watch?v=YUW3hsBH790

will be repeating often:

In my *Unremarkable Old*:

- I allowed fear to control my actions.
- I valued safety, comfort, and security higher than a life of risk, hardship or peril.
- I did *not* live to serve others.
- I was half-heartedly present.
- I was the most important person in my life.

In *The Messy, Extravagant New*:

- Love influences (and inspires) my actions.
- Risk, hardship, and peril are valued higher than safety, comfort, or security.
- Living *is* to serve others.
- I admit the half-hearted struggle and am discovering the wholehearted present.
- Jesus is the most important person in my life.

I'm appealing to you on the basis that you were designed and destined to live from a place of depth where few dare dive. Thankfully, few-in-number has never been a challenge for Jesus. The power of His message wasn't in the masses He ministered to, but the twelve He charged. They, the Apostles—the same ones who argued about who was the greatest among them or even asked Jesus if they could call down fire to destroy a village—were the ones who first adopted His message and went on to transform the world as we know it.

Jesus was and is the greatest of lovers. He was a prophet and yet so much more. The way He ignited and modeled the call to adventure wowed me during a time when I had lost all interest in the Bible, faith, and was dabbling in everything except Christianity. I'm in love with the Trinity—God: Creator, Jesus: Son, and the person of the Holy Spirit. They are my Father, Brother, Counselor—the One I'm most interested in listening to.

A devilish lie may tempt you while reading these chapters: Chad is special. He's someone with a unique gift for stepping out of the ordinary, making the uncomfortable look all too easily alluring, able even to pull rabbits out of his spiritual top hat. This is precisely why it's critically important for me to share with you that I still fall to *unremarkable old* sin. I've included successes and failures in an effort to impart to you everything I've learned about developing a life of risk, and to prove that success rarely makes an appearance without failure somewhere nearby. If God can *move* through me to touch those He so dearly loves, then I need no more evidence; He can—with equal parts compassion and power—*flow* through you. It's only grace dispensed from a good Father that any of us have made it this far. If these pages don't declare what the Holy Spirit aims to accomplish—convict sinners, empower saints—they and I will have done you no service at all.

I've included a selection of risks in the chapters that follow with the hope that my stories will serve your story. The risks with a *number* and *date* mark those that occurred during my dare, along with several taken before and after the one thousand risks time frame. Stepping out of comfort for a prolonged season was a vital start. Blossoming into and equipping you for a life of risk is what I'm striving after and praying for. *One Thousand Risks* is proof that God is still setting you up for adventure.

Jesus, come. Even now—even here—infuse my life with compassion and boldness so that You would be known more through my awkward obedience than any number of odd hesitations.

2. The Black Keys of Fear & Failure.

God whispers to us in our pleasures, speaks in our conscience, but shouts in our pains: it is His megaphone to rouse a deaf world.

- C. S. Lewis

I sat peacefully, legs crossed, on a bench facing the moon and St. John's River. A steady stream of party-goers stumbled past me toward home while I marveled at the beauty of God's creation and the ways in which Jesus had met me through the week. It was Friday, just after midnight, on Jacksonville's Riverwalk and the third night of a four-day spiritual school called *Power & Love*. The last thing I was looking for was conversation with a stranger when a man walked over and stared at the river not far from me. He began making small talk with me along the lines of how beautiful the river was at night. I agreed, and the man came closer.

Astoundingly, I began sharing deep insight over his life—specifically how he had once served as a youth leader but had been emotionally wounded from a negative church experience. He began simultaneously crying and agreeing. I prayed over him that Jesus would heal his heart and restore him to a place of deep connection with God and others. We began talking about just how odd it was that he came outside the hotel when he did and that I was sitting where I was, when I was.

Several minutes more passed and a young man walked by, turning his eyes toward ours. I greeted him, and he responded with an aloof, "Hello." Again, I found strange words slipping with authority from my mouth. "Hey man! Come over here. We need to tell you something!" Stunned, but compliant, he turned around and joined us. I began sharing what Jesus had just done, and in the same way God had given me divine insight moments earlier, the same thing began happening—but this time both myself and the man who had originally joined me began encouraging and exhorting this new friend.

Brian, our new friend, began crying and confessing his sin on the spot, sharing how far away he had traveled from Jesus. I informed him there was no time like the present to get his life right. He agreed, and the three of us held hands as he repeated a prayer to God of repentance and restoration. While praying, the bizarre thought interrupted me that Philip had baptized the Ethiopian Eunuch on the spot of his conversion[3].

I asked Brian if he had ever been baptized—marking that line in the sand to divide the *unremarkable old* from the messy, extravagant new— by expressing publicly to God, himself, and anyone else, his foremost desire to abandon all to Christ. He hadn't. "Well, would you like to get baptized out here by the river?" Brian's smile spoke loudly while his lips worked to catch up. The river would have been ideal, but it was a seven-foot drop, and who knows how deep beyond. I picked a mostly-full water bottle out of a nearby trash can, and right then and there, we poured it out over Brian's head in the name of the Father, the Son, and the Holy Spirit. He rejoiced; we all embraced. The possibility for surprises is endless in this *messy extravagant new*.

Brian's work crew had left him behind without realizing it. Stranded without his phone, wallet or anything other than the clothes on his back. Jesus reminded me of James 2:16, which says we shouldn't send people on their way without meeting their practical needs. This is where the pain problem showed up for me. I asked Brian if he would like a Greyhound bus ticket. He was shocked I offered, but all I could think about is what

---

3 The Book of Acts Chapter 8, verses 26-40

Jesus would do in a situation like this, making it harder for me to treat Brian any different than I'd treat myself. By the time we picked up the ticket, it was just past 1:30AM and Brian hadn't eaten all day. We sat down to enjoy late-night pizza when I felt the Holy Spirit prompting me to do something unthinkably messy.

Brian's bus was leaving at 6:30AM, and he had no place to stay other than outside. I had a nice four-star room with two double beds. Without thinking twice (grace and peace beyond all thoughts rational), I invited Brian to stay the rest of the night with me.

The most awkward elevator ride of my life ensued, followed by all kinds of dark thoughts, like *What if he kills me, or worse?* coupled with slightly tamer impressions: *What in the world am I doing? What have I gotten myself into? Is this Christianity? Jesus didn't say anything about this, did He?* As much as you might desire to develop a life of risk, inviting strangers to spend the night in your hotel room is likely not what you've been envisioning. It certainly was not where I had seen my evening heading.

Amazingly, Jesus instantly removed fear. I can't explain it to you, but by the time the elevator had reached the 5th floor, I was no longer afraid. Horrific thoughts of my life ending—brutal and premature—in a fancy hotel room had vanished. Just before I fell asleep, I was reminded that Brian had told me earlier in the night how he had serious back pain and physical problems. I roused to life.

"Hey Brian! Are you still awake?"

"Yeah man, what's up?"

"Do you still have pain in your back?"

"I do, it's pretty bad, about an eight out of ten."

"That's not OK. Get up, man. Jesus will heal you right now."

He stood up. We prayed. Jesus did the rest. Brian told me how insanely nuts the whole night had been, that he had never experienced Jesus like this before. I told him I was in the same space as he was. Literally and spiritually. By the time I woke up the next morning, Brian was gone and I've not seen or heard from him since.

What if this year alone every Christian on the planet took only one risk to love God and neighbor as they love themselves? I know it's an optimistic thought, but Christianity is the largest religion in the world[4], with over 2. 4 billion converts, meaning one out of every three people believes in Jesus at some level. What if love was actually the driving motivation Jesus intended for you and me?

Without a connection to God the Father, intimacy with Jesus the Son, and life by the Holy Spirit—Christianity is irrelevant, holier-than-thou, boring, empty, unconvincing, selfish, and weak. It's exactly where I had landed in my *unremarkable old*.

What I'm about to suggest is impossible—apart from divine interjection. I'm calling you to take a close, honest look at what God can do when we surrender. When I found Jesus, I was everything *but* Christian—more like agnostic skeptic meets religious Pharisee. I came with nothing but a dusty speck of hope that just maybe Jesus was who He said He was. I gave up; He gave me a new heart and a perspective so fresh I could hardly believe it. Nothing else mattered. I would go anywhere, do anything, share my story with anyone. God so loved the world that He sent Jesus, and I was happy to be His proof.

I started Christian living with zeal, passion, and expectation. I prayed, fasted and meditated often. I read my Bible like it was exciting. I led late-night Bible studies on my college campus. I loved sharing my faith. I looked for opportunities to care for people. I preached in prisons and to myself. I carried on spiritual conversations with my wife. I worshipped God with abandon every chance I got. More than anything, I dreamed

---

4 https://en.wikipedia.org/wiki/Christianity

of Jesus changing the world through me. Most of us Christians desire to know God and make Him known like *Youth With A Mission*, but for many years I struggled to love others, let alone Jesus.

What happened to me?

My guess is the same *unremarkable old* things that ensnared me, have at least tempted you…

Life.

Work.

Distraction.

Being hurt (and consequently living wounded).

Fear of others.

Fear of failure.

Fear of rejection.

Fear of God not hearing you.

Fear of looking stupid (in other words—fear of others—all over again).

In the *unremarkable old*, fear owned me. Fear, fear, fear, fear, fear, and then a few other things thrown in for good measure. Fear is the four-letter word where we suffer most. Fear marks the pain in life we all share, even every so often expose, but then mostly wish we would have left covered over. Fear is the enemy except when Jesus said, "love your enemy." Jesus did not have fear in mind. Fear has always been a feeling, like a blind guide trying to convince you how well he sees. Fear has never made for a good friend, much less a great one.

No other *unremarkable old* issue comes anywhere near threatening your true messy, extravagant potential like fear. You and I were created to carry more power than any instrument on the planet. We were designed to experience a life of risk—and the fullness of energy uncontainable—by the Spirit.

In the book of Ephesians, Paul pens this lavish reminder of what a gift

God has given us: *"Blessed be the God and Father of our Lord Jesus Christ, who has blessed us in Christ with every spiritual blessing in the heavenly places."* (Ephesians 1:3). How many blessings? Every single one. Where are they from? Heavenly places. Who delivered them? Jesus. Why bless God and Father? Because His generosity is lively and liberal.

If anything has derailed the joy in growing with Jesus and learning to love my neighbors as I desired to be loved, it has been beastly fear. There are currently 530 documented phobias[5] (how about Bibliophobia, the fear of books?). I'm not seeking to address fear in all his dirty expressions, but specifically the *unremarkable old* fear that haunts me most: fear of disapproval. Otherwise known as *fear of man* in the Bible (see Proverbs 29:25, 1 Samuel 15:24, Hebrews 13:6) and *the people-pleasing plague* everywhere else.

The premise of *One Thousand Risks* is that the fear of disapproval is most readily overcome by what I've already alluded to, and the very thing you may fear most: surrender. We obey the god we fear. In my life that god was the fear of whether or not others approved of me. Laying aside the fear of man, not by pretending your fears aren't founded, but by helping you break up with them, is what I'm after.

Jesus is faithful. He cares more for the good work He's begun in us than we ever could. *"Come to me, all who labor and are heavy laden, and I will give you rest. Take my yoke upon you, and learn from me, for I am gentle and lowly in heart, and you will find rest for your souls. For my yoke is easy, and my burden is light."* - Jesus, Matthew 11:28-30.

I learned near the end of writing this book that I should write with only a single person in mind: you. Discerning in advance that *you* would be most likely to read, and possibly even adopt, my pro-extravagance, anti-unremarkable, risk-commending manifesto. What

---

5 http://creationwiki.org/Phobia#cite_note-2

kind of person would you be? Someone already growing with Jesus or a Christian skeptic? A church-planting missionary or church-leaving atheist? Charismatic hipster, conservative Evangelical, political activist or humanitarian? Could I envision you, personally, as my ideal reader? I did envision you, my ideal reader, as a Christian (like me) living in too much unremarkable fear and messy extravagance too shallow.

My two-fold desired outcome, and prayer, for you—again regardless of where you find yourself on the 1-to-10 faith scale—is that you would be provoked to a place of fighting fear for surrendered engagement with Jesus, and that He would so inspire you to be (and then to do, no matter how messy) more than you've ever imagined. My hope is helping you see, know, experience remarkable Jesus and live the messy, extravagant expression you were born for.

Taking a risk, let alone developing a life of risk—where fighting the *unremarkable old* is a daily choice—feels frightening, nerve-wracking, and some days, straight impossible. The fear of man hasn't stopped harassing me throughout any point of this risk journey, like a thorn in the flesh that delights in punishing me. Shame and fear of failure have equally tried to disrupt my courage. The only difference between fear of man, shame, and fear of failure is the volume of their shouting. Denying each their wrongful place of influence is a lesson I'm sluggishly, but progressively learning. I close this chapter with a story to prove this paragraph.

While meeting with a friend at Barista Parlor, a Nashville coffee paradise, I noticed a group of three indie-rock-looking dudes. I felt God giving me a "word-thought" for one of them about creative value and long-term potential. Have you ever tried bargaining with God in an attempt to gain courage?

I tried telling God that if the other two got up, I'd go over and share the thought. Or if the one I felt a word for went to the bathroom I'd intercept him on the way there. I hoped I could speak to just the one privately, but that opportunity never presented itself. Before leaving the coffee shop, they were all still seated—closely together at that. I got up from my meeting and began walking out. Grace sat me down next to the indie three. I said hello, introduced myself, and awkwardly shook strange hands. They all looked at me with wide, suspicious eyes. Who wouldn't, especially considering I had just broken every rule of social etiquette?

One of the three asked me if this was some kind of Christian thing. I confirmed that indeed it was some kind of Christian thing. Dan was the man for whom God had given me the word-thought. It was more of a "mind-picture" than a word that I hurriedly shared with him. Dan's face looked puzzled, in a good kind of way. I told him I was learning to hear from God and hoped the word encouraged him. I quickly excused myself, without even asking if the word had any relevance, and walked out.

I was so scared and so often am. Probably far more concerned with how these men perceived me than I was with honoring God. Thank you, Jesus, for helping me listen and obey—even when it's awkward, messy, and my stomach is all tied up in knots. Help us help the world see how amazing You are. I like author-activist-attorney Bob Goff and his ideas on risky failure: *"People who take huge risks aren't afraid to fail. In fact, they love to fail. It's because failing means they found the edge."* He's right, though sometimes you'll feel the edge has found you.

A month or so later, I was again at the popular East Nashville espresso haven. A friend and I were waiting in line when he commented how every time he's at Barista Parlor he sees rock stars. *"Really? I don't ever notice anyone notable though it could be because I'm generally clueless."*

My friend's finger pointed to a young, bearded man wearing a jean jacket. *"Oh, that guy? He's a rock star?"* My friend nodded. "Well, that's really interesting." I told the story of how I had shared and received a word-picture for this "rock star" a while back about him feeling like he was against a creative wall, wondering whether or not he'd be able to get up and over it. My friend was now all ears. Had I known who I was sitting down with, I never would have done it. I'm praying God keeps the cloak over my eyes and yours for only seeing people as He does. Unbeknownst to me, I had sat down with *The Black Keys*, and "that guy" was their singer.

I'm going to step out here and be true to myself and this idea of living on risk. By the end of this book two major shifts will have taken place in your life: one, you will be fighting fear like never before—and you'll be winning, even if it looks messy—way more than losing. But, even when you do lose, you'll still be winning. Second, you will have grown in closeness to Jesus and have developed an ability to love neighbors that will last your entire life. Bold? Absolutely. Foolish? Maybe. Messy? Often. Extravagant? More than you know.

3. It's a Dangerous Business Going out My Front Door.

Christianity is not you being amazing, but you being amazed.

- Ray Ortlund

You've read three real-life stories (in the past two chapters) where each involved strangers engaged in conversation—by a stranger. This idea, stranger approaching strangers, might be in itself a monstrous cultural taboo for you, plain weird, or at the least an uncomfortably daunting task. I get it and fully understand all three positions. The difference between being perceived as a street salesman selling unwelcome wares, and approaching someone *with love* is two-fold:

1. We have nothing for sale.
2. Listening to, following the Holy Spirit, and reaching out to someone with a heart bent on serving them is opposite any style of solicitation.

A couple years into attending our home church, Immanuel Nashville, I overheard pastor Ray quote the phrase that our friend T. J. Tims had taped to his computer screen. "Take a risk. Your father is King of the Universe." My ears, brain, and heart nearly shut down from an overload of capacity as the weighty declaration struck a prophetic chord. I even wondered if the phrase was a Bible verse I had somehow never stumbled across.

Developing a life of risk isn't easy, is often awkward and rarely feels comfortable. The world has never been changed by easy, awkward comfort.

Why not risk? Why not cross the unremarkable line for the sake of the remarkable cross Jesus lined? The way I see it, you've already taken a risk by picking up this book and reading this far. I'm about to share many risks with you that took me about as long as it will take you to read this page. In some cases, as long as you reading this sentence. It takes about two seconds to speak out the heaviest proclamation the world will ever hear: "Jesus loves you."

God continues growing me in this messy area of stepping out of my own comfort to pray for and encourage complete strangers as a *normal* element of my Christian journey. Nothing about this idea is complicated or confounding. Yet, you will find that developing a life of risk is a rare expression. Like Asia, who I met mere moments before typing these words. She had worked for the past five years at one of Delta's many Sky Clubs.

I became the first passenger/customer who offered to pray for her. When I asked how I could pray for her, she responded by asking me to repeat my question. I did. She was puzzled, which is not an entirely uncommon response. It's okay. I offered areas where people often desire prayer—family, career paths, physical pain, relationships, world peace, et cetera. Offering to pray for those you come across daily changes everything. It changes how you see them and how they see you. Prayer offered is like not-so-secretly inviting Jesus to move powerfully in the lives of those who may never have assumed He desired to move at all. For all you know, the only god they've encountered confused them at best or hated them at worst. *One Thousand Risks* is a story of love stirred up. *"And let us consider how to stir up one another to love and good works…"* (Hebrews 10:24).

Christians are called to love *everyone* on a scale only Heaven could weigh. Jesus didn't challenge us to *argue* well with our neighbors or *despise* our enemies. He challenged us to give our lives away—even *for* enemies. When hearts crack open, thickly covered as they sometimes may appear, you've crossed a broad divide from the *unremarkable old* to the messy, extravagant new. As pastor Ray routinely sounds out around our church family, "My day is better because you're in it." Culture tilts from I/me to you/we. We're all in this together. Muslim, Hindu, Christian, intellectual atheist, super-secure agnostic, Jewish rabbi, Buddhist monk or any other image-bearer of God. No, I'm not a Universalist, but we do all share life together on this planet. Beliefs and theology aside, we are human at the core of all levels.

To help your transition from the *unremarkable old* to the *messy extravagant new*, I've filled the following pages (and future chapters) with some of my favorite success *and* failure stories. Think of them as my stories to serve your stories. Be encouraged—they're all true—but even more, if God can move through me, He can *flow* through you.

Josh's wide-eyed excitement was hard to miss as I took my business-class seat next to him en-route to Frankfurt, Germany. He made no delay in leaning over to express how this flight marked his first in "the class," his English near perfect with only a hint of German pith. I responded that it was my third, and how grateful I was for seats that transformed into horizontal beds. His eyes grew wider. I showed him the button illuminated red with the letters "Zzzz." *Press and hold this when you want to sleep.* Josh was a twenty-two-year-old health inspector visiting family in the Dallas area. We shared how we were both flying standby thanks to "Buddy passes"—airline employee passes shared with friends to travel the world. The downside to buddy passing is you are always last to be cleared. A full flight means no flight. The upside is standing top of the list for business-class upgrades on international flights.

I've grown, with admittedly *massive* room for expansion, in praying for those surrounding me—at restaurants, coffee shops, in airplanes, just about anywhere. I began still-small-praying-under-my-breath for Josh. He offered up his real fear of flying and fear of heights, two things inseparable from the other when airplanes are involved. I asked if I could pray. He nodded. I offered my hand. Offering your hand to the world is a movement as radically profound as they come.

Before landing in Frankfurt, I leaned over again and told Josh who I was (a Christian who loves God and people). I shared how Jesus had given me encouraging words specifically for him and asked his permission to share them. I like asking permission. I don't always, but it often allows people to know you're not pushing your agenda on them. Rarely will someone tell you they'd rather not hear what "God has to say." I voiced several simple thoughts on who I felt God showed me Josh was, and who he was called to be. I saw a picture in my mind's eye of Jesus warmly engaging Josh in friendship then empowering him to change the world. I asked if Josh already knew Jesus as his best friend. "No, not exactly like that. I do talk to Him sometimes." I thanked him for his honesty, and asked if I could pray that Jesus would continue revealing Himself in power. "Yes, of course." We held hands again, and I prayed what I believe to be the most dangerous prayer imaginable: "*May you know Jesus as He knows you.*"

Long before I envisioned a book, I had laid out failure and success stories from my personal one thousand risks dare on a Wordpress blog[6]. In respect for personal privacy, I've only included

each individual's first name. I've also taken the liberty of changing names or places where I sensed it was appropriate.

Like the story you just read, here's another example of a risk I took and the short summary of what happened:

---

6 www.onethousandrisks.com

[Risk No. 728, 08/07/2014]
Sarah and Spanish Ham.

My son, David, who has great taste in food wanted a Cuban-style sandwich, meaning a trip to the deli for the right bread and filling. I asked Sarah, who was helping us with the proper cut of Spanish ham, how we could pray for her. "I'm blessed, but please pray for my son who is with his father for this whole month. " I could sense pain in every word she spoke—a mother deeply missing her son and worried sick over him. We prayed, and she expressed deep gratitude. "Thank you *SO* much. That was *SO* sweet. Wow. " I felt God showing me she was dealing with neck stress/pain so I asked. She wasn't currently in pain, but I thanked Jesus for her and commanded her neck muscles to be normal. Simple. Encouraging.

The worst risk ever is not risking ever. I miss often. Not even failed attempts, downright not even trying. Jesus, help us to stop missing opportunities we could have taken. I'm not suggesting you run around all day stressing risks because eventually you'd wear out or risk-taking would end up becoming your new *unremarkable old*. This messy extravagance is about listening and following. Thank God for grace and forgiveness along the way—if you're anything like me, you'll need a steady supply of both.

People are a gift. Whether you choose to recognize an opportunity for taking risk, the person in front of you is still a gift. If you focus only on the times when you *don't* risk, discouragement will stop you from ever stepping out again. I encourage you to think of the grace-opportunities

God has already given you while quietly trusting Him to bring you many more.

I try diligently to be honest and transparent with myself when I don't risk. There are obvious times—even seasons—when I don't, and it's impossible that any human risks 100% perfectly. It might read easy to flip through these pages where God has enabled me—by grace—to step out of myself and into the *messy extravagant new*. I still struggle along. *A lot*. Be encouraged! I'm inspired by Galatians 6:9: "*And let us not grow weary of doing good, for in due season we will reap a harvest if we do not give up.*" Don't grow weary of doing what's right no matter how many times you miss risk.

Sooner or later, we have to go outside, and that's where the real wonder begins.

Jesus, help me to realize just how dangerous business stepping out my door is to the unremarkable old. Give me a greater ability to see those around me as You do. Please do whatever is necessary to grow me.

4. Intimacy and Identity Are Two Things You Can't Live Fully Alive Without.

The secret of Christianity is not in doing, the secret is in being.

- John G. Lake

If identity is a key, intimacy is the door it opens.

There was a time in my life when I knew I was a Christian, but I didn't realize I was a son. Years went by before I truly realized who I was. I believed, on many levels, that I had to earn God's attention, not realizing He had already delivered his attention—and affection—long before I even met Him. Identity is knowing who you are and intimacy is knowing who you belong to. Not only who you belong to, but who you're with—and even more—who's *with* you. *"For you did not receive the spirit of slavery to fall back into fear, but you have received the Spirit of adoption as sons, by whom we cry, "Abba! Father!"* (Romans 8:15). The whole heartbeat of Christianity is the adoption of people like you and me—once unwanted, distanced, broken, afraid. Now, living miracles. Intimacy is looking Jesus in the eyes, and at the same time hearing His voice remind you that the sum of who you are is immeasurably more than all your past-parts combined. Loneliness, depression, anxiety, fear and sins of every kind are all fading fibers compared to embracing the messy, extravagant new. Christianity—life *with* Jesus and life *through*

Jesus—is God lifting our hearts out of the *unremarkable old* and showing us that life over here is intimate belonging.

Fear always makes me feel like a hypocrite, and it's the one thing keeping us from our identity and intimacy—as sons and daughters—more than anything else. There are many times I can hear fear shouting in my head. "What if they don't get healed? Your "prophetic" word isn't from God; it's just another random thought. They will reject you and your prayer offer. What if you make an idiot of yourself? Even worse, you make a fool of God?" This is when I have to remind myself the questions and comments being shouted are all misguided. The devil and hell always ask the wrong questions hoping you and I won't ever know the difference.

The right questions to ask are: What happens when they do get healed? What if your words pierce their hearts? Yes, they might reject you for the sake of Jesus but didn't He already promise this very thing?[7] Maybe being a fool for Jesus will prove He can work with anything—even you. Even me! Take a risk, your Father is king of the universe. *"For God gave us a spirit not of fear but of power and love and self-control. The fear of man lays a snare, but whoever trusts in the Lord is safe."* (2 Timothy 1:7 and Proverbs 29:25).

Lovers are intimate, in relationship and want to be together most of all. Workers care about how much they're paid and what benefits are offered. Mike Bickle, the founder of International House of Prayer, says "lovers will always get more done than workers." Be a lover. Stay close to Jesus. Even if, or when you stray, His grace will pull you back. I have strayed—and I'm not proud of those times—but God still calls me His own and pulls me into His heart. The greatest danger in knowing Jesus is to be drawn to Him, to savor Him at first, but then to become convinced

7 The Book of John 15:18

His love is made perfect by our works. It was by grace, through faith, when you first believed. It is by grace, through faith, that you continue believing. *"If we live by the Spirit, let us also keep in step with the Spirit."* (Galatians 5:25).

If we choose to distance ourselves from intimacy because we're horrible at it, we'll only hijack the most important aspect of the Christian life. *"Not everyone who says to me, 'Lord, Lord,' will enter the kingdom of heaven, but the one who does the will of my Father who is in heaven. On that day many will say to me, 'Lord, Lord, did we not prophesy in your name, and cast out demons in your name, and do many mighty works in your name?' And then will I declare to them, 'I never knew you; depart from me, you workers of lawlessness.'"* (Matthew 7:21-23). Paul challenged us to combine our works and our faith—to be doers of the word and not hearers only[8]—but our doing doesn't necessarily make us more like Jesus. He's the one who begins and finishes our faith, and He's always game for growing us—even when we don't or can't see it. He's for your life—mess and all—your ministry and your calling infinitely more than you could ever be. Jesus is for you more than you will ever be for yourself.

I've prayed with strangers, encouraged hearts, shared word-thoughts, embraced, cried together, held hands, often reminding myself how much Jesus loves—all over the globe and in all kinds of spaces. Not only because Jesus commands me to love, but because I *get* to. That is the difference between workers and lovers. Workers have to. Lovers get to.

---

8 James 1:22

[Risk No. 360, 08/01/2013]
When Intimacy Breaks.

Spencer helped me carry a box of supplies to my car when I awkwardly blurted out, "How can I pray for you, man?" His expression quickly told me he wasn't prepared for a question this concerned. I explained how God has put this desire in me to pray for others, believing Jesus for *big* things in the lives of people like him. "Is there anything you'd really love to see God accomplish in your life?" came my rephrased and slightly less awkward offer. Spencer's response instantly reminded me of why I ask in the first place. All it takes is one response like this and I'm encouraged for days. "Please pray for my struggling and broken marriage."

I extended my hand to shake his which is when you hold on. *"In Jesus name: marriage, be restored. Relationship: be reconciled. Amen."* I invited God to move powerfully over Spencer and thanked Spencer for allowing me to pray with him. He hugged me and expressed how sincerely grateful he was for something as seemingly miniature as a prayer.

Jesus, thank You in advance for Your willingness to sweep in and restore Spencer's marriage. I pray You would restore countless marriages on the edge of disaster. Holy Spirit, please ambush broken marriages the world over with otherworldly love.

Can you imagine finally marrying the man or woman of your dreams and then not getting to know them? The hardest part about traveling is leaving my wife because there's no one on earth who I'm closer to. Marriage, apart from intimacy, is just a contract. You weren't invited to live under a contract with God, you were called to live intimately close with Him. Your connection to Him is not some formal business exchange; it's relational covenant. This is how life was meant to be with Jesus. He introduces us as his bride, his beloved, the one He most cherishes.

When our awareness of how Jesus sees us is in the proper place, both internal and external outlooks change. Everything looks different—because even when you sin or mess things up, when you don't risk or love someone as Jesus would—you're still called by His name and you can never earn more *or less* of His love.

A rarely-talked-about thief that steals our intimacy with God is *Christian-comparison,* the sin of wishing God would have made me a whole lot more like whoever I look up to most because I don't love myself enough for who He sees me as. The silence of a sin doesn't make it less offensive to God or less impairing to you. There are many in the Christian faith—and many outside of it—who I look up to. Men and women who have helped shape my faith, marriage, dreaming, interactions with family and others, how I steward finances, etc. The proper response toward those we admire is gratitude and thankfulness for the creative uniqueness in how we've *all* been wired. Confessing to Jesus that *I* struggle with being *me* is admitting the old and welcoming the *messy extravagant new.* Holy Spirit, help us be imitators of those imitating Christ.

Six Bible verses have helped me understand identity and intimacy more than anything else:

"So then, brothers, we are debtors, not to the flesh, to live according to the flesh. For if you live according to the flesh you will die, but if by the Spirit you put to death the deeds of the body, you will live. For all who are led by the Spirit of God are sons of God. For you did not receive the spirit of slavery to fall back into fear, but you have received the Spirit of adoption as sons, by whom we cry, "Abba! Father!" The Spirit himself bears witness with our spirit that we are children of God, and if children, then heirs—heirs of God and fellow heirs with Christ, provided we suffer with him in

order that we may also be glorified with him." (Romans 8:12-17).

[Risk No. 869, 05/21/2013]
God Speaks "Son" Even, and Especially, Through Horrible Choices.

I met Gabriel at the Vista County courthouse while waiting for a friend's sentencing. Gabriel was the embodiment of the Latin gang-banger stereotype if ever I've seen one. More ink covered his tattooed face than most people's entire body. I briefly heard mention of his case, and began quietly praying for him, inviting Jesus to move on his behalf.

A grueling hour and a half later, having just witnessed the hardest relational hurt in my life, I walked outside the courtroom and noticed this same Latino man waiting on a bench—Gabriel. I stooped down and told him I was praying for him, that God noticed him and cared. I asked his name and quickly prayed for him. Our eyes locked. He knew I meant it; I knew God loved him.

Identity and intimacy are the areas where I sense God desires to grow us most. Locking eyes with a complete stranger, even briefly looking into the story of their soul, inviting Jesus to meet them, is miracle-working power. I've watched people weep in front of me—purely by looking into their eyes. Often I pray in public with my eyes open, usually looking directly into the eyes of the person I'm with. Knowing I'm loved grants me courage to help others feel the same.

My heart broke as I learned the news of Tim's consideration for hiring a hitman to murder his ex-wife. [9] Friendship with Tim began dissipating around the same time I was exiting conventional music business and entering the messy, extravagant new. Though I had entirely lost touch with Tim over the years, I was utterly shocked to hear news so unlike what I had known of him. Little did I realize at the time. Over the years, Tim, whom I had known for being a strong, committed Christ-follower, had rejected relationship with Jesus—embracing an atheistic perspective in place of intimacy, or identity, with God.

A dear friend and gifted artist-pastor called me not long after news on Tim broke. "Hey man, do you know the story of this Tim guy who tried to hire someone to kill his former wife? We've got to do something to remind him Jesus loves him desperately."

"Well, yeah, actually, I do know the story, and I used to be friends with this Tim guy."

"Oh, you did?"

"Yeah, from my Tooth and Nail days—we connected often at shows and festivals—though I haven't talked to or heard from him in ages."

Despite the admittedly awkward lack of communication over the years, my friend's challenge was enough to spur an email...

May 21st, 2013:
Tim!

I have no idea whether this will even get through to you.

It's been years but you've come to heart on a near daily basis lately, and at the very least, here's a simple attempt to let you know I'm praying (as I'm sure countless thousands are). Your life is still precious to me and to Jesus. I don't think any less or different of you and I have no doubt that God is, and already has been, using even this process to reconcile

---

9 *Rolling Stone* news article, dated 05/16/2014.

your life.

I am for you. If there's anything I could do to help you, please don't hesitate. I'd be happy to hop on a plane and spend an hour talking with/praying over you. Just say the word. Anything at all, please let me know.

While I was praying for you this morning I felt God began showing me a picture of a man in prison named Bill or Billy and that he would be someone who would encourage you. I could be crazy but felt it strong enough to mention.

Jesus, I pray for my brother Tim today, that You would meet and melt him in every way that would cause him to know where You are in this process. Thank You, God, for John 14:27: *"My peace I give to you, my peace I leave with you. Not as the world gives do I give to you. Let not your hearts be troubled neither let them be afraid."*

Love,

Chad

I was shocked to see Tim's name in my inbox and assumed it must have been a manager or someone cleaning out his emails. His response came after he had been released from solitary confinement on bond and placed under house arrest.

July 5th, 2013

Hi Chad!

I finally got a chance to get this email address under control. I'm doing okay considering. Taking it one day at a time since some days are harder than others.

It means a lot to know that you've been praying for me and that you're still willing to reach out to me during this time. The man who encouraged me most in jail is the philosopher and author William Lane Craig, known as Bill to anyone who knows him personally. Without a doubt, it was his writing on some of the most difficult issues I've been pondering the last few years that gave me hope in my isolation cell.

Thank you for being an example of love.

Tim

Years have passed since the incident and ensuing worldwide news. Myself, my pastor friend, and many others have visited Tim on numerous occasions. Tim was encouraged and reminded that he wasn't alone, even when having made horrible decisions in the *unremarkable old.*

Tim lost intimacy and identity with God, resulting in desperate actions. The same can happen to any of us, including you and me.

5. By His Spirit.

Does anyone really think that America today is lacking preachers, books, Bible translations, and neat doctrinal statements? What we really lack is the passion to call upon the Lord until He opens the heavens and shows himself powerful.

- Jim Cymbala, The Brooklyn Tabernacle

Any hope of world change comes by the Holy Spirit, the Person responsible for every ounce of fruit any Christian has ever produced. So-called Jesus followers who claim to have accomplished whatever good of their own accord are pathetically deceived. How does growth develop, both in this area of messy, extravagant risk-taking and in the life of anyone desiring Christ-likeness?

"If the Spirit of him who raised Jesus from the dead dwells in you, he who raised Christ Jesus from the dead will also give life to your mortal bodies through his Spirit who dwells in you."

(Romans 8:11).

That's how. Through His Spirit who lives in us.

Through His Spirit, lost becomes found.

Through His Spirit, families relocate to countries and cities they have no natural desire for.

Through His Spirit, leaving successful music industry careers is a privilege when Jesus says, "Come, follow me."

Through His Spirit, we love enemies presently closed to the Gospel.

Through His Spirit, our mouths and hearts open when unremarkable fear tells us to stay quiet.

Through His Spirit, starving for more of God's word and presence is a gift.

Through His Spirit, learning to love God and neighbors becomes a lesson in loving ourselves.

Through His Spirit, the *unremarkable old* is forgiven and forgotten.

Through His Spirit, we *live* risk in the messy, extravagant new.

One of my most consistent prayers has been that God would give me *one* opportunity every day to love someone like Jesus does. Not in an effort to convert them, change them or rearrange them. Love simply for the sake of love, because Jesus commanded and demonstrated *love*. Some days I miss my prayer completely—those are days I apologize to the Holy Spirit. Some days I don't care—those are days I apologize to the Holy Spirit. Some days I don't feel like it—those are days I apologize to the Holy Spirit. I consistently find myself apologizing to the Holy Spirit—for not listening, not obeying, not trusting, not stepping out. He's not the kind of person who guilts us into saying sorry or doing something we don't want to. He empowers us to push past ourselves—and all things impossible along the way. "Thank You" are the words I should speak most often in connection to the Spirit. He is who shapes and sharpens my intimacy with God. He brings Scripture to mind, recalling it to me in times I require it most. The Holy Spirit illuminates God's Word and brings life beyond anything I could receive otherwise. I am empowered to step beyond myself because He is my *source*. Words come to my lips at times, and in ways, I never would have expected. Growing into the messy fullness of extravagant grace Jesus offers comes only one way: through His Spirit.

You might be praying and considering the idea of becoming a full-time missionary to some foreign place and people. That's a massive risk. Maybe you are making an effort to notice strangers, smile, or even give a little more of your time. You may just be hearing of risk-taking for the first time and are not sure this is for you. Regardless of where you're at, there's always room for growth in Jesus. No matter *who* or *where* you are, I'm placing this practical dare in front of you: Ask the Holy Spirit to empower you toward loving someone like Jesus does. Maybe you ask him to lead you to one person a day, a week, a month, a year—but I dare you, no matter how cliché or oversimplified you think this might be— ask the Holy Spirit to help you love someone else the way Jesus loves. You can't pray a prayer bigger than God can handle.

If God can move through me—someone who still deals with fear, insecurity, doubt, anxiety, despair, and all the same old unremarkable impediments—He can clearly *flow* through you. Ask the Helper for help and then begin taking risks no matter how huge or tiny they may seem. Through His Spirit.

"Therefore, since we are surrounded by such a huge crowd of witnesses to the life of faith, let us strip off every weight that slows us down, especially the sin that so easily trips us up. And let us run with endurance the race God has set before us. We do this by keeping our eyes on Jesus, the champion who initiates and perfects our faith. Because of the joy awaiting him, he endured the cross, disregarding its shame. Now he is seated in the place of honor beside God's throne. Think of all the hostility he endured from sinful people (like me); then you won't become weary and give up." (Hebrews 12:1-3, with my added emphasis).

The stories that make up this chapter deal with times where the Holy Spirit worked in such a way that the outcome would not have been anywhere near the same without His help.

[Risk No. 935, 10/09/2014]
Caught Largely Unaware.

While standing outside the church for a special night of worship in San Jose, Costa Rica, my Colombian pal Joani and I heard the obvious crying of a young child not far from us. We turned our heads counter clockwise and noticed a couple frantically pushing a stroller around in circle after circle. Not wanting to overthink the experience, but feeling compassion all the same, we stretched our hands toward the child and began praying.

Seconds later, our mutual friend Sam jet-streamed out of the venue toward us saying, "Oh, are you guys praying for the boy? Do you want to come pray over him with me? We think it's a *demonic* thing." I wasn't sure what to think of Sam's statement, but Joani and I followed him over. We introduced ourselves to the parents, and I asked if the boy (who was three) was still teething. Having had two children of my own, that seemed a natural possibility. "No. He has been like this since yesterday at about midnight."

There's no way for me to easily describe what this boy was doing other than furiously *freaking* out. I've never seen anything like it. My first thought was that if we didn't see breakthrough in prayer, these parents needed to dial Costa Rica's equivalent to 911. This was one of those times I wished a camera had been nearby. Intense is an exaggerated understatement.

I asked the parents, as crazy as my suggestion seemed, if I could try holding the boy. They were happily relieved to hand him off. There I held him, swaying to the deafening noise of screaming child. I prayed over the boy and gently rocked him while he screamed his worst, teeth digging into my left shoulder. Surprisingly, he did calm down ever so *slightly*. At some point while holding this little boy I began sobbing. I was in Costa Rica, holding a hurting child who represented so clearly to me—in that moment—all the broken unfairness of the *unremarkable old*. I wept with God's heart of compassion. The group prayed for what must have been more than ten minutes while I awkwardly cried and cradled the screaming child.

As soon as Sam and Joani were done praying for the parents, I felt a strong sense of authority come over me. I clearly and confidently *knew* what had to be done. I began rebuking specific demonic names as the Holy Spirit gave insight. Spirit of idolatry, witchcraft, sexual immorality, etc. Each name I rebuked resulted in the little boy coughing—as though he was expelling the invisible. Though I had seen the ministry of deliverance happen before, never had I witnessed demonic influence over a child. I was fairly shocked. Six or seven names came to me, and every time the boy coughed as I rebuked the spirit by name, commanding it—in the name of Jesus—to leave and not return. I asked the Holy Spirit if we were done, and within seconds, a powerful peace came over the boy, and he instantly stopped screaming. Entirely—not *even* a whimper. I handed him, quiet as grace, to an overjoyed, grateful mother.

Sam shared with me that, prior to coming to Jesus, this couple had lived a wild life. While Sam and Joani had been praying over the couple, they discovered the child's grandmother was a practicing witch. She despised, even cursed, the couple's coming to Jesus.

Rarely will the devil leave without a fight and this had been just that. I felt anguish in a way I never have. Jesus won. The Holy Spirit helped. No power of darkness is any comparison to the love of God. It seems blatantly unfair that the devil would attack even a helpless child. The devil doesn't care. "*The thief comes only to steal and kill and destroy. I came that they may have life and have it abundantly."* (John 10:10).

[Risk No. 539, 01/08/2014]
Nurse Catora.

I picked up several last-minute supplies before heading home for the night. As I checked out, I wasn't thinking about how to pray for the cashier or how God might feel about her. On the way out to my car I felt convinced I had not taken advantage of every opportunity. Keep in mind, conviction is very different than condemnation. Conviction turns you around, imparting grace for the otherwise impossible. Condemnation weighs like a brick around your neck, convincing you you're worthless.

Freshly inspired, I ran back inside and shared with Catora how I felt God had wired her. Her face shone. I asked if she was considering being a nurse. She was! I prayed a blessing over her life and her pursuits to care for others. I drove home feeling grateful for the Holy Spirit's ability to help.

Several months later, and again I found myself overwhelmingly surprised by the Holy Spirit. He's always amazing, of course, but at times I have to shake my head in wonder at His abundant kindness. Beth had asked me to run into the grocery store nearest to my office. Low and behold, there was Catora—the girl God had given me crazy insight over about her future in nursing. She remembered me. I remembered her, and asked how things were going in nursing.

Catora began explaining how as soon as she finished her shift she would be going in for her first interview, but that she had an uneasy feeling about it and felt as though she wasn't supposed to take this first opportunity even if she was offered it. I asked if we could take it to Jesus. "Of course!" We held hands and invited the clarity of Jesus to permeate and disrupt her uncertainty.

As I turned to leave she commented, "You know, it's really crazy that I haven't seen you for months and the very day that I have to make a major decision, God sent you back to me. " So crazy. *Lord, thank You.*

[Risk No. 741, 08/11/2014]
Prison Potential.

Again, Joani and I had the sweetest of privileges, this time in visiting a local Nashville prison. My friend started a non-profit ministry here in town, called Send Musicians to Prison, and had collaborated with many amazing Nashville artists on a beautiful concert inside a local prison. All the musicians involved wrote songs inspired by the inmates' journals they had recently written over a study on the beatitudes (from Jesus' Sermon on the Mount). Powerful. While there, Jesus gave us many opportunities to pray.

Ponce was an inmate with a serious spinal issue. He was wheelchair bound and in tons of pain. I asked if I could pray for him and he kindly agreed. I commanded pain to leave and for any metal in his body to dissolve. By the end of the night I discovered Ponce had *zero* pain. He shared with me a dream from two nights prior where, in the dream, the metal disappeared from his body, and his back was healed. I'm convinced God sent me to prison, on this specific day, purely for Ponce.

Anthony had a left knee problem evidenced by the crutches he was holding. We prayed with his permission. Left knee problem healed. A man with right knee pain came alongside Anthony. He walked over when he noticed us praying for Anthony and hiked up his knee. "Back issues?"

"Yes." Back issues healed.

I shared a word about how God had wired Yoshi. We hugged, she seemed super encouraged. We prayed for Steve's shoulder/right side and encouraged both him and his wife. An inmate from Honduras had a patch on his eye from an accident involving a slingshot. I commanded the eye to be restored. We didn't have enough time to find out if he was instantly healed as security escorted us out. I talked with a security guard on the way out and asked if he had a left knee issue. "No. It's my right knee. " I asked if I could pray. "Sure. " We prayed. Pain left.

A female security guard I talked with on my way out had back issues and leg problems in the form of compressed discs. I prayed and encouraged her. I met two more security guards right before I walked outside who were talking about how tired they were. I walked over, asked for their hands and prayed for them—without asking permission. Sometimes grace is so thick there's no need to. I said to one, "I see you like the energizer bunny. " She began crying and laughing at the same time with the oddest look on her face. "That's crazy; my nickname at church is the energizer bunny!"

Thank You, Jesus, for revival in prison and everywhere else. May there be continued outpouring of the Holy Spirit that no amount of distraction, skepticism or unremarkable convenience can stop.

Take a risk; your Father is King of the universe.

6. Awkward Awesome.

Be, and then do. Doing to be is backwards.

- Todd White

Why should you—or I, or anyone else for that matter—even bother with the outlandish concept of risk? If you're at all like me, you'd far prefer a life of stability where you are always the victor. Fortunately, Jesus offered the heartbeat of risk-taking primarily to stop us from living for ourselves so we could begin tasting glory in His now and forever kingdom:

And one of the scribes came up and heard them disputing with one another, and seeing that he answered them well, asked him, "Which commandment is the most important of all?" Jesus answered, "The most important is, 'Hear, O Israel: The Lord our God, the Lord is one. And you shall love the Lord your God with all your heart and with all your soul and with all your mind and with all your strength. ' The second is this: 'You shall love your neighbor as yourself. ' There is no other commandment greater than these." And the scribe said to him, "You are right, Teacher. You have truly said that he is one, and there is no other besides him. And to love him with all the heart and with all the understanding and with all the strength, and to love one's neighbor as oneself, is much more than all whole burnt offerings and sacrifices." And when Jesus saw that he answered wisely, he said to him, "You are not far from the kingdom of God." And after that no one dared to ask him any more questions. (Mark 12:28-34).

Developing a life of risk is worth the hassle because nothing spells *'You shall love your neighbor as yourself'* more than actually treating someone the way you would want to be treated. Christians were called to a standard of living—for and toward others—at a level that demonstrates genuineness, compassion, care and the power of God. Though Jesus has taught me (and continues to teach me) many things since beginning this risk extravagance, the point I'd like to share with you now is that people are exceptionally valuable, regardless of how they treat you or make you feel.

A great filmmaker friend of mine coined the phrase, "awkward awesome," as a description for my experiences in learning to love stranger-neighbors. He's right. Any attempt you make to love/encourage/heal/give/prophesy-over someone will always go one of four ways.

Your *messy extravagant* moments will:

1. Start awesome / Stay awesome.
2. Start awesome / Turn awkward.
3. Start awkward / Stay awkward.
4. Start awkward / Turn awesome.

I've tried applying each of the above categories to the stories in this chapter so you get a feel for what to expect on your own risk-taking adventure.

Rarely will a moment start awesome and then turn awkward. Most of the time you will find they start a bit awkward and end surprisingly awesome. People have asked how much I was charging for my prayers—crazy, I know! They've asked what church I attend (in an attempt to either discern how wacky I am theologically *or* because they're genuinely curious). Shawn Bolz, the Los Angeles-based spiritual adviser and minister, puts it this way when it comes to hearing from, and growing with, God; "*One of the steps to getting more and more from God is to be faithful and to take a risk even when it feels like what you have is insignificant or silly.*"

One time, two older, well-educated, Hasidic Jewish men in Istanbul agreed to pray with me only *after* I pointed out that Jesus and all the early apostles were Jewish. That was sweet of the Holy Spirit to bring to mind the beliefs we hold in common and I felt incredibly honored to pray with these men. (Started awkward / Turned awesome.)

On one occasion, I asked a young Universalist lady from Seattle seated next to me on an airplane if I could pray for her. She mistook my request, responded by saying she wasn't sure how, and as I offered her my hand, she began "praying" some form of a sincere, well-intentioned, positive vibe over me. I quickly realized what had happened but didn't know how to stop her without making matters worse. I returned the favor and we had a splendid Jesus conversation at 30,000 feet. (Started awkward / Turned awesome.)

[Risks No. 186-201, 04/08/2013]
Risks Taken North and East.

Right as I walked into the Nashville airport (BNA) I noticed a man in a wheelchair. I asked if he was in pain. Quite the contrary, he was simply relaxing in the comfortable seat of an otherwise empty wheelchair. I laughed, and headed for security. While in line for security, God *highlighted* one of the TSA agents in a way where he simply stood out to me a bit beyond the ordinary. I approached the man and gave him a quick, encouraging word. At first he had no clue what I was about to say, then, after I shared, he warmed up to me. (Started awkward / Turned awesome.)

Demetrius and Mike were standing around BNA's inner terminal waiting for a customers' shoes to shine. My cloth Vans were unfortunately not made for shining. However, God did give me encouraging words for both Demetrius and Mike which then opened the door for a special hand-holding prayer time. I offered, and missed, a "word-thought" over them about back and shoulder pain. (Started awesome / Turned a bit awkward).

As I rounded the corner to head down the terminal, I stopped Michael with a huge brace on his right knee. I asked what had happened. Rugby accident resulting in six serious surgeries. I offered to pray and he warmly received. Michael wasn't in pain but seemed surprisingly grateful that I would offer. (Started awesome / Stayed awesome).

I was on the phone a few moments later when I walked past a smiling woman out in front of a fifteen-minute massage spot. I walked by and whispered, "Your smile is a blessing. " Her smile widened. You will begin noticing how much a difference smiling makes. If the only lesson you take away risking from this book is an authentic smile, I'll still be thankful. (Started awesome / Stayed awesome.)

Milly was one of my airline stewardesses aboard a flight out of Nashville. I offered her a word about joy, and asked about her left shoulder and arm. I was correct on joy, wrong on the shoulder or arm. I was still graced with the favor of praying over her. Rarely is someone expecting you or I to "call out" whatever ailment they have, so if, like me, you miss word-thoughts, simply ask how else you can pray. (Started awesome / Turned awkward).

Scott was my neighbor on a flight headed to the Northeast. I sensed God giving me thoughts about his work and how fellow-workers perceived him at work. I also felt he was facing interoffice conflicts that God wanted to set straight. He seemed surprised when I shared the above and was wide open to prayer. I also sensed I should ask about his lower back, but couldn't quite bring myself to do it. (Started awesome / Turned awkward).

Shawn and Lauren were neighbors to me on my second, and final, flight of the day. I shared encouraging words of identity with both and was able to talk extensively about what God has called me to. They listened intently, and allowed me to pray together with them before we landed. (Started awesome / Stayed awesome).

Once on the ground, I rendezvoused with friends for dinner. Lauren was working as our waitress at the pizzeria. God gave me insight into her having the heart of a dreamer and having a ton of compassion for others—specifically called into nursing. She stepped back, mouth agape, and shared how she'd been wondering if she should go into nursing. We prayed over her hurting back though I completely missed a word-risk about pain in her knee. (Started awesome / Stayed awesome).

Cara and her friend worked at Starbucks for our post-pizza stop. I sensed Cara's friend was a team player, and asked if either of them had back pain. Cara did. I prayed for her, and she noticed no change. Instead of praying again, I allowed unremarkable fear to sway me. Forgive me, Abba Father. On the way out of Starbucks, I spotted a lady with a large neck brace. She allowed me to pray for her though no obvious or immediate change took place, which is not my way of saying nothing happened. It's possible *everything* happened outside our short couple of minutes together. We encouraged her and went along our way. People with obvious physical conditions/disabilities/problems are a clear opportunity for reaching out. Simply offering prayer proves care in a way the individual may have never experienced otherwise. (Started awesome / Turned awkward).

I struck up a conversation with the man working behind the counter when we stopped at a gas station for late night snacks. He wasn't interested in us praying for him or discussing Jesus. It's OK, we prayed for him once we got back into the car. Regardless of whether it's awkward, awesome, both, or neither—it's not about me (or you)—the journey is learning to love others despite the odds of failure or rejection. "How can I pray for you?" is a question that will often serve as your starting step between the unremarkably common and the extravagantly supernatural. We all have needs, some of us seemingly more so than others. Every need matters to God and does not escape His notice. Jesus loves opportunities to meet needs. He's waiting to walk with you through uncomfortable spaces His Spirit is confidently comfortable with. *"By this is love perfected with us, so that we may have confidence for the day of judgment, because as he is so also are we in this world."* (1 John 4:17). (Started awkward / Stayed awkward).

The next morning, we met friends at a local diner. The owner, Dan, was a Christ-follower and all around friendly, boisterous New-Englander. We prayed for and encouraged the ministry God had placed in him. I perceived a mental picture of Dan opening more diners and asked if that made sense. It did, he had just been thinking about purchasing a diner long closed in another section of town. (Started awesome / Stayed awesome).

Judy was our sweet, quick-witted waitress. Welcome to the Northeast! God gave me a word-thought about her left hip and knee. I was beyond encouraged when I learned I was right (she also had screws and a metal plate in her right foot). I prayed and told her to give the prayer a little time. I'm not sure why I suggested the idea of giving prayer time, but that's what felt most natural in the situation. Listening to the Holy Spirit and your own heart is the way forward in developing a life of risk. On the way out, I asked how she was feeling. Her words poured with genuine shock as she informed me her hip felt entirely better and her foot was mostly better. I prayed for her foot a second time (praying more than once for the same need is something I do often especially where progressive, rather than immediate, improvement is occurring) and was able to remind her how much Jesus loved her. She said she'd already been talking to Dan about Jesus. (Started awesome / Stayed awesome).

Caroline sat directly across from me in the diner. I heavily felt in my heart God's compassion for her to the point that when she got up to leave, I awkwardly followed her out. I told her God wanted to remind her how He felt for her. I prayed for her, and God gave me a word about her back, which He kindly restored on the spot. (Started awkward / Turned awesome).

Sonya was one of my airline stewardesses on the trip back home. I was way off base on a word about her neck and shoulders. Still, I was able to pray a blessing over her despite having been wrong. Renee was another stewardess on the same flight. God gave me a picture of her delivering balloons to children and that she had a sweet gift of generosity. Before I shared, I told Renee that God had given me a picture. Her immediate response was, "UH, OH!", insinuating that whatever the picture was would be anything but good. Amazing how many people consider God for His anger or judgement first—His love and mercy last. (Started awkward / Turned awesome).

While seated toward the back of the airplane, I wanted nothing more than to close my eyes, nap, listen to worship music, and maybe read a book. Before boarding, my eyes had been drawn to a young man wearing an orange shirt. This same young man sat down in the aisle directly across from me. To my surprise, no one took the aisle or middle seats next to me. Before taking off, I felt God giving me a strong impression that this young man was facing a royal challenge and to remind him that God would help get him through it. Amidst being tired, and not wanting to talk, I felt God's persistent nudge.

I relocated from the window to the aisle seat to be closer to the young man. I introduced myself and shared how I was a Christian, and I believed God had given me a word-thought for him. Upon sharing this thought, the young man instantly acknowledged the relevance of it.

Maurice and I ended up talking for nearly two hours. Turns out Maurice was a youth pastor studying to become a pastor. His father had passed away only months prior, and he'd been struggling to stay on course for his July graduation. Jesus flowed through Maurice to wonderfully encourage my heart and used me in doing the same for him. (Started awkward / Turned awesome).

Maurice and I landed in Nashville and began walking toward baggage claim together. On the way, I noticed Al and his wife looking at a bright yellow Harley Davidson motorcycle on display. Al was in a wheelchair. I told Maurice we should see if they would allow us to pray for them. We approached, and I commented about how shiny the bike was. They agreed. I asked Al if he was in pain and he joked about how his wife was his true pain. I asked if we could pray for him and he agreed. It was beautiful. I held his hand and Maurice laid hands on his shoulders. We prayed, commanding his body to be restored, welcoming God's presence to minister to both Al and his wife. I was in a hurry and didn't have Al test his body, but peace covered my heart. The couple thanked us for caring. (Started awesome / Stayed awesome).

Indeed, one minute you can be perfect strangers and the next feel like long-lost pals reunited. The kingdom of heaven is a vast, beautiful community of those drawn near who were once far off. I excitedly arrived home to family and took them out to our favorite wood-fired pizza where Ashley was our waitress. Initially, I wasn't receiving anything from the Spirit. Toward the end of our dining-time, I thought I discerned a message about Ashley studying overseas. I was way off. Nor did she have pain in her right wrist. Nor did she "need" prayer for anything. I had just experienced God's presence so strongly in the Northeast and the first moment back home was about as awkward messy as they come. *I love you, Jesus. Please draw Ashley closer to You. Thank You for her.* (Started awkward / Stayed awkward).

[Risk No. 15, 01/08/2013]
Mary hates drugs.

I moseyed around the store feeling disheartened and not really wanting to pray or step out toward anyone. I invited God to change my attitude. As I was checking out, I struck up a conversation with Mary who was in her late forties/early fifties. I asked how her back and shoulders were feeling from all the standing. "Oh, they bother me all the time but I go to a chiropractor. I won't take drugs, I hate drugs. "

Cool, I don't like drugs either. "Mary, God has given me *gifts for healings.*"

"Wow, that's cool. It's like something you can give out?"

"*Yep, exactly. It's not meant for me, it's meant for others. May I have your hand?*"

Mary extended her hand, and I prayed God would bless her year and give her godly goals. I commanded pain to leave her back, shoulders and neck. I told stress to leave and she immediately tensed up. "Wow, I can totally feel this weird sensation when you told stress to leave, stress is a big one for me. " As I began to walk away, Mary looked at me and then thanked me—especially for the fact that I looked her in the eyes while I prayed. (Started awkward / Turned awesome).

Whenever I experience more awkward than awesome, miss "word-thoughts," or avoid risk altogether, I'm reminded that making messes out of obedience to Jesus far outweighs never attempting anything extravagant in His name. Anytime you experience failure *or* awkward while risk-taking, weighty discouragement will tempt you. Ask God to forgive you for potentially making a mess and thank Him that no mess is too big for His cleaning.

Only two things matter when you walk away from a risk taken, regardless of how strong or poorly you feel it goes: 1. Was the person valued for who they are, or for the potential they carry? and 2. Did you attempt to love? It's not uncommon shortly after a failed risk to see a wonderful breakthrough. God is good. Keep looking up. Thank Him for the great times and the not-so-great times.

Obedience is worth the awkward and the awesome.

7. Heal.

*Bless the Lord, O my soul, and all that is within me, bless his holy name!
Bless the Lord, O my soul, and forget not all his benefits, who forgives all
your iniquity, who heals all your diseases, who redeems your life from the
pit, who crowns you with steadfast love and mercy, who satisfies you with
good so that your youth is renewed like the eagle's.*

- Psalm 103:1-5

The first time I ever witnessed Jesus healing someone through me was
in Albuquerque, New Mexico with *The Glorious Unseen*, an ambient
worship artist I had signed back in my record label days. The band
invited me on stage to share whatever God had placed on my heart. I
distinctly recall hands on my shoulders and prayers supporting my
pre-stage steps. Friends had graciously begun interceding for me—still
a Christian music industry man straddling the fence of *unremarkable
old* and the *messy extravagant new*—moving way outside the realm of
comfort. God's manifest presence (an experiential, euphoric sensation of
wonder and clarity in perceiving God's nearness) was so heavy that all I
could think to do was drop to my knees and shout my heart out to God.
One of the prayers I spontaneously uttered was "healing" over the city
of Albuquerque. This was not the kind of specific healing-command I've
grown into praying these days. My prayer was more of a hopeful longing
for everything wrong being made right again.

At the end of the night, I wondered what kind of impact my praying
words carried. Several people approached me, but two stood out most

excitedly. The first was a leader in the Albuquerque hardcore scene and a staunch atheist. This young man claimed to literally have *felt* God's power. With tear-filled eyes, he asked me to pray Jesus would redeem his soul.

Second was a young lady who had come to the event on crutches, suffering from a dislocated kneecap. During my naive prayer for healing over hurting Albuquerque, she sensed her kneecap switching and shifting back into place. Rightfully shocked, she began placing weight on her leg, discovering that her knee was completely healed. Before approaching me she had been running around the venue—san crutches—in total awe. She hugged me and thanked me for praying. My inner-skeptic wondered what in the world I had done.

"What do you think God's heart for healing is?" That was the heavy question I was asked by a good friend while sitting outside a small-town hotel at 3:30AM. At the time, I viewed healing as mysterious, confusing and mostly perplexing. Still, my friend's question was fair and well-intended. My response spun on the heels of the one thing I had known best: experience. *Very rarely* had I seen Jesus heal the sick. Notice, I emphasized the words *very* and *rarely*—like the first and strange time I had seen a young lady on crutches healed in Albuquerque.

Growing up believing that gifts of the Holy Spirit were hardly in operation, I had not a clue as to the enormity of God's heart toward healing. I responded to my friend's question the only way experience had taught me. God *occasionally* heals, but He *mostly* doesn't. He's mysterious, working in often equally mysterious ways. My friend coolly, but confidently suggested I ask God to share His healing heart with me. I obliged, asking God to show me how He feels about sick, hurting, poor, broken, beaten people. This was when the mystery of *healing* began unfolding to me. I place this same question now before you. Negative and positive experiences aside, would you consider asking Jesus afresh to share the Father's heart for healing with you?

Holy Spirit, would You show me—in the name of Jesus—the heart of God for healing, in all it's beautiful forms? Healing of pain, sickness, disease. Healing of heart, soul, mind, strength. Healing in broken relationships. Healing of emotional and psychological disorders. Ultimate, forever healing leading toward salvation—oneness of God and man through the blood of Jesus. Please remove from me the hurts I've sustained and the walls I've built up in this area because of my experiences, or lack thereof. Show me, not by inexperience or unbelief, but by the Word, how to treat others the way Jesus would treat them, regardless of how far this revelation may take me from comfort and into risk.

Within two weeks of praying my quirky healing prayer question, I noticed a bizarre Facebook message. It came from someone I had never talked to before. The message started out saying the Holy Spirit had placed a thought on this obedient sender's heart. I was directed to investigate an included link, pointing me to an audio series titled, "Divine Healing Technician Training" broken into *nineteen* one-hour-ish segments. Like anyone, I was a cynic on high alert. One, trust had not yet been established between us. Two, links coming by way of Facebook messages are rarely valuable. Three, *NINETEEN* hours of teaching from someone I'd never heard of with a title as bizarre as this? I was 99 parts skeptic to 1 part curious. This couldn't possibly be Holy Spirit work.

Driving from Nashville to New Jersey—toward yet another music festival with reluctant *Come&Live!* staff in tow—I informed unsuspecting friends of the intriguing Facebook message. Curiosity took over. I asked if we could listen to the first five minutes so I could clear my obnoxious conscience. We spilled out of the rental van fifteen hours later having made it through nearly *fifteen* of nineteen sessions. Years after that drive to New Jersey I can tell you that I have yet to see everyone I pray for instantly healed, but I can also share with you that I've seen more people healed, more frequently, than ever before in my life. I have experienced, first-hand, Jesus—the Great Physician—caring for more physical, emotional, spiritual problems than I ever knew existed. This is a short list of only some of the areas I've seen Jesus healing, restoring, resetting:

1. Hearts
2. Plantar Fasciitis
3. Achilles tendons and ankles
4. Knees, legs, hips
5. Resetting broken toes and fingers
6. Backs (including disc issues & scoliosis)
7. Eyesight (blindness, glaucoma, nearsightedness, farsightedness, degeneration)
8. Headaches, migraines, sinus issues, neck problems
9. Shoulders, wrists, elbows
10. Hearing loss (total and partial)
11. ME/Chronic Fatigue Syndrome
12. Lyme disease/Youth arthritis
13. Bladders, urinary tracts, digestive systems
14. Reproductive issues, ovaries, uterine problems
15. Brain, Portal vein and stomach tumors disappearing
16. Skin issues
17. Sleeplessness
18. Allergies of various sorts
19. Diabetes
20. Emotional/Psychological problems - depression/anxiety/phobias

Note: One of the first signs that an instant healing miracle is occurring is when an individual begins experiencing something out of the ordinary (excessive heat, radiating warmth, cooling, electricity, even pain worsening or suddenly moving to another part of the body). It's not always the case that they feel something, but often they do. Either way, if you have a heart to see people healed, don't let feelings dictate what you believe about who God is and how He feels about those around you.

Stories in this chapter deal with two sides of the same coin. The first side includes evidence of miraculous healing to glorify God, help you understand why I believe as I do, and encourage your faith in Jesus, the Great Physician of yesterday, today and forever. The other side of the coin covers problems, or issues, that I've dealt with in believing Jesus desires to heal others along with experiences that are helping me grow beyond those problems. I pray they do the same for you.

[Risk No. 280, 05/21/2013]
The Deceitfulness of My Fleeting Feelings.

I go through seasons where I don't feel much like praying for others at all, when my life is more messy than anything extravagant, or new. I don't know what exactly hinders me, or what exactly will hinder you— probably pride, fear, distraction, becoming overwhelmed by how many sick/hurting people need healing, or all four combined. There may even be times where you think about giving up on risks altogether, healing or not. Progressing always requires more courage than retreating does. God is kind; He will increase your faith and keep you moving. This is not a game of numbers or how to make a quick return on short-term impact; this is the messy *way* of love. When love floods over—possibility is anytime, anywhere.

I noticed Cheryl walking alongside an alley wall as I returned to my parked car, stuffed from lunch at The Pharmacy Burger Parlor. She was using the wall to support the weight of her body in a labored attempt at walking. Her face spelled pain. I walked over and asked if she was indeed in pain. "YES!" shot out quick and frustrated. I shared how God had given me a heart for the hurting and asked if I could pray. She filled me in on the experience of extreme pain in both hips and how surgery was scheduled later in the month. I asked Cheryl to place her hands on each hip, and then I gently touched her hands. "*In Jesus' name; hips be healed. Bones: be restored. Body: work properly.*"

Pain immediately left the right side and the left became noticeably better to her. Cheryl began weeping while I continued praying over her. She then motioned to her mouth and said she was supposed to have serious dental work due to bacterial growth. She asked if I could pray for her mouth. "*I'd love to! Bacteria: leave! Mouth: be healed!*" As is the case with many people I've had the joy of praying with, I never saw Cheryl again and don't know whether her dental problems were supernaturally healed.

Life is never fully expressed based on what you or I *feel*. Life is about inviting Christ's love to flow through us, even when we don't know how the chapter ends. We're the least likely hands and feet Jesus could have ever chosen as His own. But He chose us all the same.

[Risk No. 375, 08/22/2013]
Being Jesus Is Usually More Listening Than Talking.

I met Wonda at the register of a home improvement store. She was wearing a black elbow guard on her left arm. I asked what the problem was and then listened. So much of being Jesus is in the listening. Wanda explained how she had an issue with her tendons brought on from all the required heavy lifting. Her pain level was significant (eight out of ten), and when I offered to pray, she said, "Here!" quickly placing her left arm directly in front of me.

I spoke only three words; "*Elbow: be healed.*" I instructed Wonda to try moving her elbow around and asked where the pain was on the scale. "Zero!" Left elbow healed and one thrilled employee. I blamed the entire, beautiful moment on Jesus. Wonda proclaimed how amazing He is and how grateful she was for knowing Him.

[Risk No. 469, 11/06/2013]
Something out of Nothing?

Larry was selling pre-Thanksgiving Indian corn and miniature pumpkins on the east side of highway 70, heading away from Nashville. I noticed him while driving past. Larry was in a wheelchair and missing his left leg from the knee down. I thought to myself as I continued driving, *Why wouldn't you stop on your way back and pray for him?* Well, in reality, several things will keep you from risking in general. Especially in cases like this. Risks are rarely convenient. The *unremarkable old* has taught you to place greater premiums on convenience than treating others how you'd love to be treated.

I've prayed for a handful of limbs to grow back—not grow out, which I've seen on many occasions—I mean extraordinary creative miracles, *something* where there is currently *nothing*. What I have not seen would love to keep me from what Jesus does see. Throughout this journey, you will have to ask God to help you be more like Jesus; He's the only way forward. One of the reasons the Holy Spirit is here is to answer "help-me-be-more-like-Him" kind of praying.

"Believe me that I am in the Father and the Father is in me, or else believe on account of the works (the miracles Jesus performed) *themselves. Truly, truly, I say to you, whoever believes in me will also do the works that I do; and greater works than these will he do, because I am going to the Father. Whatever you ask in my name, this I will do, that the Father may be glorified in the Son. If you ask me anything in my name, I will do it. If you love me, you will keep my commandments. And I will ask the Father, and he will give you another Helper, to be with you forever, even the Spirit of truth, whom the world cannot receive, because it neither sees him nor knows him. You know him, for he dwells with you and will be in you."* (John 14:11-17, with my note on *works*).

On my way back I pulled over and purchased mini pumpkins. By grace, I asked Larry about his leg. Diabetes. I inquired whether he still had diabetes. He did. I requested to pray two crazy prayers over him. First, for diabetes to leave his body completely. Second, for his left leg to reappear and grow back 100% normal like the right. He looked at me funny. "Well, I guess so." We prayed and I invited Jesus to become all the more famous in and through Larry. We didn't see his leg grow back on the spot. I did drive away knowing in my heart that stopping was a whole lot closer to Jesus than ignoring.

[Risks No. 519 & 520, 11/22/2013]
The Blind Will See.

Our family stopped off at former Steel-city stomping grounds of

Birmingham, AL to visit old friends. While sipping Octane coffee together at a local park, we noticed two women walking not far from us. One had thick, black glasses and a blind walking stick with a tennis ball attached to the bottom. She used the walking stick to feel the ground in front of her while holding the other woman's arm. I told my friend that we ought to ask if we could pray for and with them.

We did, and they were surprised. At first. They allowed us to pray and I began commanding Sheila's eyes to see again. The word *command* sounds threatening and packed with authority—like forcefully instructing a dog to stop barking. Early in the Father-heart-of-God search, I scoured Bible verses where Jesus begged or pleaded when it came to healing and deliverance. The only time I discovered Jesus pleading with the Father was immediately before His journey to the cross.

I sensed Sheila might be dealing with degenerative eyesight and asked. She was. I rebuked degeneration of the eyes. In the moment, I felt significantly tempted not to have her test progress, for fear progress tested would be expectation too loudly spelled out. I ignored temptation by asking how Sheila's eyes felt and whether she noticed any change. "Well, I *can* see you more clearly!"

"Wow, really?"

We prayed over Sheila's eyes twice more and both times even greater improvement came.

"I can see much better on this side and all that cloudiness is gone."

Jesus gave my friend and I pointed prophetic insight over Sheila and her daughter, DeAngela. At one point, Sheila began crying, hugged my friend and said, "You just told me everything I was talking to God about last night!" Both mother and daughter were massively encouraged and we ended up spending fifteen minutes together as though we had been friends for fifteen years.

As we parted ways, I watched at first as Sheila was still holding her walking stick out in front, but the tennis ball wasn't touching the ground. Several moments later, Sheila and DeAngela caught my eyes again. This time, Sheila was walking with the cane tucked under her arm pointing it *up* and *behind* her with absolutely no assistance from her daughter at all. She was walking perfectly on her own.

The pages of this book are aimed mostly at teaching you how to develop a life of risk, where the heart of *One Thousand Risks* marks the bold conviction I've adopted since my 3:30AM hotel conversation. The answer to my prayer petition came not in the form of principles, theories or especially arguments. My answer came in the form of a Person. When I asked God how He felt about healing, He pointed me to Jesus. I asked Him about all the common objections to healing like Job, Paul's thorn in the flesh, Timothy taking wine for his frequent stomach issues, Trophimus left sick or why only one man was healed by the pool of Bethesda. He always responded with the same answer. The Word made flesh—Jesus.

Everything Jesus embodied served to represent the Father's heart for humanity. If you want to know *who* God is, look to *how* Jesus lived. I know it might sound crazy to you, but it is that simple. "*He is the radiance of the glory of God, the exact imprint of His nature. He upholds the universe by the power of His word. After making purification for sins, He sat down at the right hand of the majesty on high.*" (Hebrews 1:3). If you're anything like I was—clueless toward God's heart for healing—ask Him.

I close this chapter with stories from South America. Travel may be one of the most absurd gifts to enter my life through the non-profit ministry work I do with *Come&Live!*. In the case of this story, it was our team's second time traveling to Bogotá, Colombia—a city of twenty million inhabitants with a history rich in Latin culture and drug cartel violence. The first time Colombia was mentioned I recall all of us thinking, "don't they kidnap people like us there?"

I awoke early to the feeling of weighty discouragement—thanks to all our camera gear having been stolen the day prior—until my friend asked me to accompany him to the corner bakery for coffee. I'm always down for espresso and sweet South American pastries. We met a man in his fifties standing outside the panaderia. Cesar had been a construction worker eighteen years ago when a brick fell two floors down causing irreparable disc damage to his back.

When we met Cesar he was severely hunched over, required a cane for stability, and couldn't walk without extreme pain. We prayed twice and his pain began to diminish. We asked him if one leg was shorter than the other. It was. Thanks to the sweet bakery we were able to borrow a step stool, sit Cesar down on it, and verify his right leg as shorter. We commanded his leg to grow. It grew. He was 100% healed on the spot, able to walk without his cane. For the first time in eighteen years, he stood perfectly upright. For the first time in his life, he gave his heart to Jesus. Joy replaced whatever discouraging thievery the devil had up his sleeves for me.

Later on the same trip, I met a precious woman, who couldn't afford doctors, that for years experienced a hard mass growing in her stomach, causing present pain. We prayed over her with a team of our Colombian friends, and she reported that the pain had instantly vanished. She began actively digging her fingers into her stomach in an attempt to locate the former mass—to no avail. Where it went? No clue.

Shortly after this happened, a handsome, well-built young man told us he desired to be right with God after having just witnessed his mother's stomach being healed. He was reconciled to Jesus—the most profound healing miracle that ever has, is, or will take place—and then asked his mom for her forgiveness toward the way he had treated her. With several local pastors united together with us, this once rebel was baptized on the spot using a bucket full of Amazon river water.

On an unsuspecting Tuesday night in the former drug cartel strong-hold of Medellin, Colombia, We dropped to our knees or laid prostrate before the Lord as God's glory swept over us during an extended time of worship in a small, humble church. A young man, An, approached me asking if I would pray for his 12-year-old cousin who had a problem with his right eye. It was here in this atmosphere of worship that I met Anderson.

We began praying, and I began testing progress by holding my fingers up, at random, not more than a foot or so in front of him. At first it was obvious Anderson was just guessing—and guessing wrong. Then, slowly, Anderson began seeing my upheld fingers more consistently. I would have him close his left eye and look around the room. To his surprise, he was seeing colors. Anderson's vision continued to improve with each round of testing. Our film-maker friend instructed Anderson & An to ask Anderson's mother to verify what we were witnessing. By the time contact had been made with Anderson's mother, he was reading my fingers with 100% accuracy and was calling out specific items—watches, shoelaces, t-shirt emblems—not just colors in general.

I informed the group that Anderson's mom was coming to validate and confirm what we were all witnessing, but it wasn't until after the service that she & Anderson's uncle arrived. Near instantly the whole crowd that had wandered mostly outside came rushing back inside. I greeted mother and uncle, then asked if Anderson was her son. He was. I asked whether he had an eye problem in his right eye? Yes. But not only had he experienced a vision issue, he was born totally blind in his right eye due to optic nerve issues. At this point, I stood stunned. Born blind? The entire time praying for Anderson I had assumed some form of vision impairment, nothing close to blindness from birth.

I asked Anderson's mom to test his vision and placed my hand to close his left eyelid. His mom said, "No, it's not that eye, the other one."

For seconds masquerading as hours, confusion hit me, and my heart sank thirty floors into the ground. Had I been praying for the wrong eye this whole time? Oh God, his mom is here, this crowd is anxiously awaiting, and I feel shame on too many levels to count. How could I have done this? I didn't know what else to do so I began praying for Anderson again—buying myself time to crawl out the back door.

Anderson's mom pulled out the first object, a knitting needle. Anderson did struggle a bit to see it. He said it was long & slanted up at an angle, but he didn't convince mom. I could feel skepticism creeping up in her and I realized that it wasn't doubt as much as the protective nature of a mother. If we had duped her son, she'd be the shoulder he would cry on. Next, she pulled a water bottle out of her bag and the dialogue went like this:

Mom - "What's this?"

Anderson - "A water bottle."

Mom - Surprised, but still not quite convinced: "How much water is in it?"

Anderson responded, motioning with his fingers; "Only a little bit at the bottom, the label looks like this and the cap is this color."

Instantly the room roared in uncontainable celebration, a mother held her arms wide for a son restored, and I dropped to my knees crying praises to God, weeping in gratitude.

Obedience is ours; results are God's.

*Several of these stories were captured in the *Come&Live!* documentary, Colombia [Esto Es Reino / This Is Kingdom] which is available free of charge on YouTube. [10]

---

10 https://youtu. be/y7HfCN0YqAU

8. Side A: Praying in the Present / Side B: Joy in the Journey.

Rejoice in hope, be patient in tribulation, be constant in prayer.

- Romans 12:12

Gavin Coffee was our loss and Heaven's gain. Gavin died young, passing both suddenly and unexpectedly in a freak car accident north of Seattle, leaving behind his beautiful wife and five incredible children (one of whom had yet to be born). I had the privilege of attending City Calvary Chapel with Gavin. Many traits Gavin bore stood out to me as exceptional. One Gavin-characteristic has transferred me from the *unremarkable old* to the *messy extravagant new* unlike any other. If you told me right now you were only willing to take one piece of advice from my whole book; please take this one.

Without fail, Gavin's response to every care or concern I would share with him—no matter it's significance—was always met with the same response. "Let's pray. Right now." Gavin would stop conversation midstream, place his hand on my shoulder, and invite God to meet me on the lines of which I had just shared. One time I asked where Gavin had learned this prayer strategy. His answer proved simple and sincere, reflections of who he was. Gavin went on to explain how if he didn't stop to pray in the moment, he would likely tell someone that he'd offer to pray for them but then walk away forgetting. He desired his yes to be *yes*. And do you know what? He always made me feel cared for and highly valued. Do this one thing for others especially when they share a need—or when you see/sense a need present—and you will know the *unremarkable old* is shrinking.

If you're still unsure whether Jesus is real, or if He actually loves you, then I applaud your bravery for being present here with me. So much of my risk story has been me following Gavin's lead. I couldn't possibly recount how many hundreds, likely thousands of times, I've asked strangers and friends alike if I could pray for them right then, right there. Not because I'm a spiritual guru but because Gavin took time for me and reminded me not to forget. Rarely are prayer-offers met by sighs of public insecurity (like, dude, please keep your Jesus-faith private) but mostly they're met by the sweet openness of bewildered smiles.

Christianity is believing Jesus cares—hears—and invites us to *"come boldly before the throne of grace, to receive mercy and find grace in your time of need."* (Hebrews 4:16). I've included the next two stories because they represent praying in the present, and how much the idea of present-praying has changed the way I view my relationship to God and others.

Here's one of the wilder examples of God's grace *and* praying in the present: When I had the privilege of meeting Daniel, several friends on our ministry team had already begun praying over him. Earlier in the night, I had noticed him entering our conference in Bogotá, Colombia with a unique sort of limp that curiously caused me to wonder what had happened. Out of nowhere, a thought flashed through my brain; *whatever is wrong with him is too hard for God, don't even offer to pray.*

Compassion and the concept of *praying in the present* drew me to push through, asking Daniel if he would be willing to tell me his story. Daniel shared with us how six years prior he had been caught by his pastor having sex with his pastor's daughter. His pastor—her father— stood knocking at the door to the apartment while they scrambled to find a place to hide Daniel. Instead of owning up and admitting what was happening, they decided that escaping through the window was the best choice. In the fluster of the moment it seemed the right idea, even though the apartment window was *six stories* up. Daniel and his girlfriend hurriedly tied sheets together that he could use to rappel down the side of the building.

Once out the window, Daniel watched in horror as the knot in the first set of sheets began unraveling under the weight of his body. The knot gave way completely, and Daniel recalled how his eyes scanned the sky rolling in slow motion while his body did a complete flip in a motion anything but slow. Daniel smacked the concrete pavement six stories below while his girlfriend shrieked in pure disbelief. Hearing commotion and all the screaming, her dad broke through the apartment door and ran to the window only just barely saving his daughter from jumping out the window after her boyfriend. Daniel's pastor—his girlfriend's father—rushed downstairs to find Daniel bruised and beaten, but unbelievably still breathing.

Though Daniel was in complete shock, adrenaline had taken over, and he began profusely apologizing to his pastor for what he had done. The pastor wrapped his arms around Daniel saying, "Don't apologize to me, apologize to God." And that's what he did, saying "Lord, please accept my soul today in paradise, forgive me for what I just did. I would like to be with You eating by Your side, but if You want to give me life again, I'll accept the pain. . . " His pastor prayed over him, and Daniel believed he was dying, describing an otherworldly peace like the sensation of his spirit departing from his body. Daniel arrived at the hospital a quadriplegic, paralyzed from the neck down—but shockingly—alive.

The doctor's had no hope that he would survive longer than a day. Daniel's mom is a nurse and was by his side the entire time. Daniel, though paralyzed and in excruciating pain unlike anything he had ever experienced, recalls his mom weeping and praying through the night.

When I asked him if his mom ever thought he would walk again, he looked up at me, smiled and said, "Yeah! She knew I would walk again. She was always honest with me and told me, "If you wanna walk you need to focus on God and your rehabilitation. More discipline and faith, Daniel." By the time we met Daniel, six years after the accident, he had fully surrendered his life to Jesus. Through a combination of prayers and physical therapy, he stood literally a walking miracle.

Offering, or even being asked, to pray in the present may not always feel spiritual in the moment. Make no mistake, it *is*. Daniel *still* had pain in his hip and leg, which disappeared completely on our first round of prayers for him, though he experienced limited control and range of motion over his right foot and leg. We prayed over him again and had the joyous privilege of walking a whole city block with him—the first time in six years where he walked without assistance of any form. We collectively praised God for undeserved mercy and grace. Daniel's mission in life is to help prove the kindness of God to anyone willing to listen - especially when we sin, when we try hiding our sin, or even when we try escaping through six-story windows.

Jesus, I pray you empower Daniel to communicate his heart with honest transparency while he seeks to write words and chapters in his own book. Bless the work of his hands for Your glory.

[Risk No. 151, 03/06/2013]
Blinding Grocery Store Glory.

Another example of praying in the present was when Beth and I stopped by Trader Joe's to pick up a few groceries. We briskly made our way through several aisles when I noticed a man in a wheelchair near the coffee. He seemed to be loudly talking to someone, very much alive. I turned around and thought to myself, *Should I offer to pray for him? Now?*

Beth instructed me to get in line while she grabbed a few extra supplies. She returned, and somewhere along the way, I found courage. *"I need to go pray for the man in the wheelchair."* I went looking down the aisles, finding Jeff and his family in the frozen foods. Jeff was smiling expressively while talking to a little boy. I approached him and, as promised, the Holy Spirit gave me words to speak. I shook Jeff's hand while telling him his joyful demeanor inspired me. He seemed moved. I introduced myself to his wife and daughter, and we talked about how we ended up in this city. They were from Los Angeles, living in Memphis, but working their way toward Nashville.

Jeff shared how six years ago he had been suddenly hit with a disease (multiple sclerosis) resulting in the loss of feeling in his legs among other issues. I told him about Jesus and what He had been teaching me and that I wanted to pray for him. He agreed. I knelt down and took his hands in mine. Before we even prayed I noticed the redness of his eyes and tears beginning to form. I prayed against the disease, against any plans of the enemy, and commanded his legs and body to operate normally again.

I may have prayed for 60 seconds, probably less, but I recall quietly thanking God for the grace to pray with authority over a condition I wouldn't naturally have had faith for. I opened my eyes, looked up at Jeff, and noticed tears streaming. Then, bewildered, I noticed two older men with their hands on Jeff's shoulders, one on the left and one on his right. Both men immediately went their separate ways, neither whispering even a word. Jeff began talking about how God had sent him angels that day. I told him how I was simply learning obedience to Jesus in my *messy extravagant new.*

I hugged him and praised God for him. In the end, I completely spaced on asking Jeff how he felt physically. Thankfully, he did give me his business card. Later in the day I emailed him to ask how he was doing. This was his unedited response.

OK, so to answer you exactly; I DID FEEL SOMETHING MAN!!! Firstly, I did feel something; the power of prayer because, oddly enough, for our family's 3.5-hour drive home, I didn't have any pain in my legs nor any uncontrollable muscle spasms in my legs. I was driving, and didn't have to stop for my incontinence issues and that usually doesn't happen!! I can hardly do a 45-minute stint of driving without either happening.

I felt OUR brothers there in prayer, together. . . MY ENTIRE FAMILY FELT THAT JUICE, THAT POWER FROM GOD. . . Those were angels in physical presence—do not mistake what happened. My daughter insists on drawing what she says she saw; she saw the light from above, she saw all of our wings; she mentioned an "aura of blinding light" and my wife agreed and said the whole mood/vibe in the entire store flat changed and for the better—they felt warm in His graces.

I will likely never know this side of Heaven whether we were hosting angels unaware, but I know God moved that day. I also know He'll provide you with grace for the impossible.

Thank You, Jesus.

Side B: Joy in the Journey.

This chapter is titled with a Side A and Side B because I've always liked the idea of vinyl records which consist of an A side, B side and a forced pause between the two. Additionally, I believe that praying in the present is closely linked with experiencing joy in, and throughout, the journey.

One of the common mistakes I've made is rushing ahead into ideas or opportunities without having first sought time with Jesus. I'm a seven— "the Enthusiast"—on the Enneagram personality test. I enjoy travel. I love experiencing culture, nations, people I would never have imagined visiting. If I'm not careful, I'll make my own way and assume God is following *me*. David from the Bible, that epic failure and success of a man after God's own heart, said it like this: *"My soul, wait silently for God alone, for my expectation is from Him."* (Psalm 62:5). Waiting on God doesn't mean you're waiting alone. Unlike praying in the present, waiting on His directive means you begin watching for the *what, when, where* and *how* of His moves.

I spent years in the music world knocking on doors and finding ways to grow career success. It's not necessarily wrong to be a doer. When I quit my career for full-time ministry, I made a promise to God and myself. I promised not to route my own course. My prayer was, and is, that I would be primarily empowered to follow. And follow well. What good would come from claiming all Jesus had done if ultimately, I had been a great marketer of my own agenda? God hasn't called you to grow a ministry; He's invited you to seek first His kingdom and His righteousness.

Releasing *joy* over life's journey is something I could never do apart from Jesus. Joy is fruit of the Spirit and fruit of walking close to God. *"The joy of the Lord is your strength. Rejoice in hope, rejoice in the Lord. Consider it pure joy when you endure trials. May the God of hope fill you with all joy. Ask, and receive, that your joy would be full. A joyful heart is good medicine. The kingdom of God is not a matter of eating and drinking but of righteousness and peace and joy in the Holy Spirit. But the path of the righteous is like the light of dawn, which shines brighter and brighter until full day."* (Various Bible passages). Sailing away from the *unremarkable old* into the messy, extravagant new without hoisting up *joy* is like smashing holes in your hull while simultaneously wishing your journey a bon voyage. When joy is in short supply, invite God to lift you closer to His perspective. He will. Joy will find you.

The experience that follows highlights just how crucial joy in the journey is when nothing seems to be going the way you want—or believe—it to.

[Risk No. 977, 12/31/2014]
Kidney Stones. . .

I had no idea that within minutes of arriving at my in-laws' home for the New Year's celebration of 2014, I would be faced with one of the more painful challenges of my entire life. It all began when a weird cramping sensation struck my abdomen. Short moments later, a sharp, distinct pain hit my right lower back. I excused myself from family and performed a mostly frantic, slightly optimistic Google search by typing in, "tips for quickly passing a Kidney stone." No Google tip came to my aid. I hardly slept that night due to constant, agonizing pain to the point of repeated vomiting. Hot baths helped ease the pain momentarily, but nothing removed it—no amount of rebuking, walking, commanding, sitting, agreeing, kneeling, Bible-quoting, worshipping or friends praying. Everything I knew to do in praying for sick others seemed to provide me with nothing in the immediate other than trusting I was going to seek and praise God despite the less-than-exciting circumstances.

By mid-morning the next day, I visited the local Emergency Room where they gave me fluids and meds that finally knocked out the pain along with a CT-scan of my right kidney, which I *later* discovered would cost me $6,000 out of pocket. Indeed, two stones were present. One was passing through the kidney, and the other was still securely lodged somewhere further north. I thought to myself while in the ER that I should offer to pray for waiting, hurting people but couldn't get to a point where compassion for others trumped my own dizzying experience. I was released, prescribed a high dose of pain meds, and felt much better that afternoon. That night I dozed off and on—mostly off—as pain ramped up again. I was still praying, rebuking, worshipping, thanking. Times like these are the true test of 1 Thessalonians 5:16-18: *"Rejoice always. Pray without ceasing. Give thanks in all circumstances for this is the will of Christ Jesus for you."* God's will is me giving thanks—regardless.

We decided to drive home the following day to get the kids back on routine and me to my bed. I hadn't thrown up in several hours so we risked the drive. Thankfully, we made it with little trouble other than me looking like the horse and rider of pale death. I laid down for a nap and awoke an hour later, stunned. The pain, in grim ferocity, began stabbing my right side like it was pure fun and games. I couldn't believe neither meds nor prayer were able to contend with this pain. I circled our living room what must have been hundreds of times, attempting to control my breathing, hoping pain would miraculously pass. It didn't. Enter trip number two to the ER *here*.

Arriving at St. Thomas Hospital was mildly relieving until I learned a grueling two-hour admittance awaited me. I took more meds (which lowered my pain from a 10 to a 9. 5 on the pain scale) and then paced outside in the cold. I began prayerfully complaining something along these lines: *God, this is pathetic. I don't know why this is happening right now but it would be way better if I at least had the heart to pray for others who are here. At least give me a story out of this pain.*

Within seconds, a couple rounded the corner right to where I was pacing. Jared and Anne were looking for a break from the freezing, windy evening to light a cigarette. I asked why they were there. Anne had experienced a minor heart attack and had a history of heart issues in her family. I told them how I had just complained to God about my issues and not having the joy to pray for others. I asked if I could please pray that her heart issues would be healed. "Uh, sure…," was enough for me to instruct Jared to place his hand on his wife's heart. I began praying and instantly sensed the Lord's presence. I finished seconds later and watched tears streaming down Jared's face. "Man, that was real. Nobody ever does that anymore. " I smiled and encouraged them with God's love. Anne wasn't experiencing pain in the moment. Then Jared turned and began praying over my kidneys. I was blown away by his kindness to pray over me though I didn't sense an ounce of instant physical relief.

A few minutes later, I found myself praying over Bill (and his wife) who was dealing with excruciating pain in his groin with no clue as to why. The Holy Spirit moved in a powerful prayer time—especially considering I was equally suffering. I was able to pray for my doctor, my nurses, and received a prophetic word—followed by sweet hugs—for one of the ladies cleaning up patient rooms to make room for more patients. Me, The Holy Spirit *and* morphine were quite the peculiar trio that night.

My pain reminded me of the compassion Jesus had, and has, for the hurting. I confessed my compassion and joy had been waning. I had not sensed as free or as caring as I knew I had been called to be. I was finally released from the hospital, driven home high-as-a-kite-on-morphine and loaded up on fresh fluids. Still, a smile in my heart sprouted greater than the testing/affliction/call-it-what-you-will of what I had just endured.

As a result of the kidney stones ordeal, I canceled my first (and only) trip of the year—ten days in Australia ministering with *YWAM* friends. My heart was heavy at the idea of bailing on such a special opportunity, but I sensed in my spirit, as did the doctor, that it was wisdom to rest. One of the amazing—and hilarious—ways in which God wonderfully works? I received a near-full credit from my flight cancellation, allowing me to rebook a trip (with the same group two weeks later) while they were on mission to New Zealand.

"And we know that for those who love God all things work together for good, for those who are called according to his purpose." (Romans 8:28). While in New Zealand, I had a number of wild experiences that even brought me to weeping tears one morning, praising God for His persistent faithfulness in the midst of pain unlike anything I've ever experienced. What the enemy means for evil, God turns to good. I was in severe pain for two short days. What God delivered beyond pain was profoundly grander, including:

1. Spending unrivaled time with my good pal, Stevie, and his second year *YWAM* students in Auckland, New Zealand (one of my favorite cities on the planet).
2. Being the only speaker privileged to share at two festivals taking place during the exact same weekend.
3. Hanging out with many incredible artist friends from all over the world.
4. Meeting my now friend, and brother, Dave Schenk. Through Dave, meeting his wife, Ness, and their whole beautiful family.
5. Being invited by Dave to speak and share my heart at what would become Easterfest's (Australia's largest Christian festival) final offering.
6. Visiting Australia not once—but twice—in the same year.
7. Hanging out and loving others alongside one of my fathers in the faith, Todd White. One of the highlights of my life was being able

to baptize and pray for a bunch of youth together during *Sleeping Giant's* set.

8. Being on the same flight "randomly" out of Auckland with Todd (and a bunch of Nashville bands) then hanging out and loving alongside Todd at LAX. I recall asking whether Todd ever missed words of knowledge. "Oh, dude! All the time! I just ask the Father why I missed it anytime I do." Todd, and my unplanned, unscheduled time with him, was a dear gift.

9. Meeting with close friends whose marriage had been suffering. Praying/crying with a husband and wife divided by the struggle of life.

10. Running into, and praying/prophesying over, an actor who played the lead Uruk-hai orc in J. R. R. Tolkien's *The Lord of the Rings* (more on this in chapter 11).

In addition to all the above, my year proved the busiest twelve month travel season of my life, with a total of seventeen trips on five continents in partnership with *Come&Live!, Steiger International* and *YWAM*. In a matter of months, I went from mostly sitting in the back of airplanes to largely sitting at, or much nearer, the front. What the devil meant for evil (Kidney stones/pain/confusion/trip cancellation) God indeed flipped for good. These trips meant something truly special because I didn't ask for them nor did I see them coming. God poured out sovereign kindness as a reminder that He is greater than any problem I could ever face.

Don't underestimate His ability to restore and reconcile you. Keep looking up and thank God for any and every opportunity to pray in the present as you seek greater joy in the journey.

9. In Keeping with Humility, the Kingdom, and its Gifts.

Pride is a form of cosmic plagiarism—claiming to be the author of something that is actually a gift.

- Timothy Keller

The Holy Spirit gave me a word of knowledge when I was teaching at a *YWAM* base in Newcastle, Australia at the end of 2015. The "word" was that someone present was deathly allergic to apples. Until the morning I shared the "death-by-apples word" I had no clue it was even possible for anyone to have an allergic reaction to fruit, especially apples.

Little did I know three students in a class of 60 were all highly allergic to apples. We prayed as a group for each of the three apple-allergy students, and each felt led of their own accord to try eating an apple, which under normal circumstances, would have resulted in anaphylactic shock.

Thankfully, EpiPens and a registered, practicing nurse were both with us. The student with the worst reaction took the first bite (she was also the most intent on eating an apple) followed by the other two. In the end, all three were instantly healed. The girl with the worst reaction called her mom who wasn't a Christian. After hearing her daughter's story, she prayed with her over the phone to receive Jesus. One way Jesus is speaking to me in the now is by drawing me to the notion that gifts and fruit—without intimacy or humility—is twisted. *"By this my Father is glorified, that you bear much fruit and so prove to be my disciples. As the Father has loved me, so have I loved you. Abide in my love."* (John 15:8&9). Bearing fruit—delivering to Jesus everything good He deserves from our messy lives—is impossible if we try producing apart from abiding. One of my prayers throughout this season has been that Jesus would produce fruit in my life in keeping with humility and that I would notice fruit more obviously in others *and* in myself. I've been inviting the Holy Spirit to continue breaking down areas where I'm hard, where I don't care for God or others, where I lack compassion. I pray repeatedly that God would break my heart for the lost, for the sick, the poor—anyone who goes consistently unnoticed. Until we learn to abide in the love Jesus has for us, fruit will never be what it could be because we'll be striving for attention or affection—or both. The life most likely to recognize attention and affection from Jesus is the life abiding closest to the heart of the Father. If I don't abide, I fail, regardless of how much "fruit" might look outwardly appealing. *Jesus, thank You for fruit, especially fruit that lasts. Help me bear the kind of fruit that will be most pleasing and satisfying to You. Teach me to abide. Amen.*

I know Jonathan Edwards, the Puritan revivalist, mostly for two things: *Sinners in the Hands of an Angry God* (a classic sermon he preached) and his thoughts on spiritual pride. My spiritual pride scares me more than sinners in the hands of an angry God. Yes, God is jealous, and He is just. Yet it was His kindness that lead me to repentance (Romans 2:4). Listen to Jonathan Edwards (circa 1741) on the foundation that gifts and fruit of the Spirit were always meant to stand on:

The first and worst cause of errors that abound in our day and age is spiritual pride. This is the main door by which the devil comes into the hearts of those who are zealous for the advancement of Christ. It is the chief inlet of smoke from the bottomless pit to darken the mind and mislead the judgement. Pride is the main handle by which he has hold of Christian persons and the chief source of all the mischief that he introduces to clog and hinder a work of God. Spiritual pride is the main spring or at least the main support of all other errors. Until this disease is cured, medicines are applied in vain to heal all other diseases. It is by spiritual pride that the mind defends and justifies itself in other errors and defends itself against light by which it might be corrected and reclaimed. The spiritually proud man thinks he is full of light already and feels that he does not need instruction, so he is ready to ignore the offer of it.

On the other hand, the humble person is like a little child who easily receives instruction. He is cautious in his estimate of himself, sensitive as to how liable he is to go astray. If it is suggested to him that he is going astray, he is most ready to check into the matter. Nothing sets a Christian so much out of the devil's reach than humility and so prepares the mind for divine light without darkness. Humility clears the eye to look at things as they truly are. Psalm 25:9—He leads the humble in justice, and He teaches the humble His way. If spiritual pride is healed, other things are easily corrected. Our first care should be to correct the heart and pull the beam of pride out of our eye and then we shall see clearly. [11]

If humility isn't the thickest coat warming my messy, extravagant new, odds are I've already gone astray.

My pastor is full of classy one-liners. By the sweetness of God's grace he likely doesn't even realize what profundity enters His heart and exits his lips. I will never forget this line Pastor Ray delivered one Sunday morning: *There is no Christianity without humility.*

I can't think of a bolder, more pure example of humility than Jesus— willing to lay aside His heaven to enter our hell, proving humility at the greatest level the world will ever witness. His humility stirs me to live low. I will say it again; I love 1 Corinthians 14:1 - *"Pursue love, and*

---

11 http://www.grace-abounding.com/Articles/Sin/Pride_Edwards.htm

earnestly desire the spiritual gifts, especially that you may prophesy." I also love the counterweight to this verse found in the first few sentences of 1 Corinthians 13; *"If I speak in the tongues of men and of angels, but have not love, I am a noisy gong or a clanging cymbal. And if I have prophetic powers, and understand all mysteries and all knowledge, and if I have all faith, so as to remove mountains, but have not love, I am nothing. If I give away all I have, and if I deliver up my body to be burned, but have not love, I gain nothing."*

My heart hungers for *more* miracles, signs, wonders, powerful gifts of the Spirit. But I'm certain Jonathan Edwards, the apostle Paul, or any mature Jesus-follower would agree, all gifts are fruitless efforts if they aren't accompanied by love *and* humility. Desiring one without the other is meaningless. Gifts are wrapped for a reason. They represent the surprise we pass along to those we cherish—the one we've spent time, thought, energy and money on. Gifts, small or large, say what we often don't. The person possessing the gift makes the investment deliberately to pass it along. Spiritual gifts are no exception. Any gifts the Holy Spirit delivers to you are meant to be wrapped and delivered to someone greatly treasured.

The gifts of the Holy Spirit are mentioned several times in the Bible, with the most common reference being 1 Corinthians 12:4-11:

"Now there are varieties of gifts, but the same Spirit; and there are varieties of service, but the same Lord; and there are varieties of activities, but it is the same God who empowers them all in everyone. To each is given the manifestation of the Spirit for the common good. For to one is given through the Spirit the utterance of wisdom, and to another the utterance of knowledge according to the same Spirit, to another faith by the same Spirit, to another gifts of healing by the one Spirit, to another the working of miracles, to another prophecy, to another the ability to distinguish between spirits, to another various kinds of tongues, to another

the interpretation of tongues. All these are empowered by one and the same Spirit, who apportions to each one individually as he wills."

By now you have heard me frequently mentioning terms like "receiving a word," "missing words," "prophesying over," and idioms like "word-thoughts" and "mind-pictures." These all spawn from two different spiritual gifts, what the Bible considers treasures from the Holy Spirit: *the gift of prophecy* and *the gift of words of knowledge.* I can best explain these gifts, along with *the gifts of healings* to you—the three gifts I exercised most through-out the one thousand risks window—by giving you examples, from chapters 4 and 5 in the Book of Luke, where Jesus applied each.

1.) Prophecy involves encouraging, building up, exhorting, speaking truth over someone's potential or reminding them who they are called to be. In Luke 4:16-30 Jesus enters his hometown of Nazareth, opens the scroll to the prophetic book of Isaiah and reads aloud these words:

"The Spirit of the Lord is upon me, because he has anointed me to proclaim good news to the poor. He has sent me to proclaim liberty to the captives and recovering of sight to the blind,to set at liberty those who are oppressed, to proclaim the year of the Lord's favor." (Luke 4:18&19).

The local hearers don't realize just how radically prophetic these words ring until Jesus makes a bold, audacious claim about who He is and why He's on the planet:

"Today this Scripture has been fulfilled in your hearing." (Luke 4:21).

In the example above Jesus prophesies over Himself, not someone else, though usually this gift is delivered from one Jesus follower to the next. Sometimes the simplest, most profound prophetic words, are to speak God's Word over someone in a supernaturally direct and applicable way.

2.) Words of knowledge is a gift where the Holy Spirit empowers us to know something about someone's current condition/situation that we could not have simply guessed, usually in connection to their condition/

situation being healed or rectified. This story out of Luke chapter 5 illustrates Jesus knowing something supernaturally about a situation that He was about to repair—at the same time confirming His identity as the Messiah:

"On one occasion, while the crowd was pressing in on him to hear the word of God, he was standing by the lake of Gennesaret, and he saw two boats by the lake, but the fishermen had gone out of them and were washing their nets. Getting into one of the boats, which was Simon's, he asked him to put out a little from the land. And he sat down and taught the people from the boat. And when he had finished speaking, he said to Simon, "Put out into the deep and let down your nets for a catch." And Simon answered, "Master, we toiled all night and took nothing! But at your word I will let down the nets." And when they had done this, they enclosed a large number of fish, and their nets were breaking. They signaled to their partners in the other boat to come and help them. And they came and filled both the boats, so that they began to sink. But when Simon Peter saw it, he fell down at Jesus' knees, saying, "Depart from me, for I am a sinful man, O Lord." For he and all who were with him were astonished at the catch of fish that they had taken, and so also were James and John, sons of Zebedee, who were partners with Simon. And Jesus said to Simon, "Do not be afraid; from now on you will be catching men." And when they had brought their boats to land, they left everything and followed him. " (Luke 5:1-11).

3.) Gifts of healing is where a person is divinely healed through prayer, and usually (though not always—think the apostle Paul's handkerchief or the apostle Peter's shadow) involving physical touch (the laying on of hands). [12] Back over in Luke chapter 4—and throughout all four Gospel accounts—Jesus operates powerfully in the gifts of healing to help people

---

12 Luke 4:40.

see and know that He is exactly who He claims to be, the only Son of the living God:

"And he arose and left the synagogue and entered Simon's house. Now Simon's mother-in-law was ill with a high fever, and they appealed to him on her behalf. And he stood over her and rebuked the fever, and it left her, and immediately she rose and began to serve them. Now when the sun was setting, all those who had any who were sick with various diseases brought them to him, and he laid his hands on every one of them and healed them. And demons also came out of many, crying, "You are the Son of God!" But he rebuked them and would not allow them to speak, because they knew that he was the Christ." (Luke 4:38-41).

How and why am I convinced that God intends for Jesus-followers *now* to apply the gifts of the Holy Spirit? This is possibly the greatest question pertaining to spiritual gifts a skeptic of any kind, Christians included, could ask. Like so much in the kingdom of God, it's simple. Jesus instructed His own disciples to use the gifts:

"And he called the twelve together and gave them power and authority over all demons and to cure diseases, and he sent them out to proclaim the kingdom of God and to heal." (Luke 9:1&2).

Ok, sure, but that was over two thousand years ago and these were *the* capital A twelve apostles, right? Absolutely correct.

Look at the great commission:

"Now the eleven (Judas had hung himself) disciples went to Galilee, to the mountain to which Jesus had directed them. And when they saw him they worshiped him, but some doubted. And Jesus came and said to them, "All authority in heaven and on earth has been given to me. Go therefore and make disciples of all nations, baptizing them in the name of the Father and of the Son and of the Holy Spirit, teaching them to observe all that I have commanded you. And behold, I am with you always, to the end of the age." (Matthew 28:16-20, comment mine).

Do you see the connection? In both Scripture passages Jesus gave commissions:

1. Proclaim the kingdom of God and heal
2. Make disciples of all nations
3. Baptizing them (all nations) in the name of the Father, Son, and Holy Spirit
4. Teaching them to observe all I have commanded you

The final commandment Jesus gave to his closest, most devout followers was to teach disciples from all nations to observe all He commanded them. So, what then, did He command them? Proclaim the kingdom of God and heal (among many other critically crucial instructions like "love your enemies"[13]) and teach every new Jesus-follower (us) to proclaim the kingdom of God and heal. It is as simple as it sounds. Jesus preached the kingdom of God and healed. He commanded His disciples to preach the kingdom of God and heal. Finally, He commanded His disciples to teach us *all* He had commanded them, like preach the kingdom of God and heal.

We can either open the gifts God gives us and spend a lifetime enjoying them, growing in them, learning about them or we can shove them aside for something that "sparkles" finer. *One Thousand Risks* is my celebration of gifts that were meant to be opened, embraced, practiced and shared. My attention is directed mostly to prophecy, words of knowledge, and healing because those are the gifts that most often help me love my neighbors a whole lot better.

The stories you're about to read in this chapter capture risks involving one or more gifts of the Spirit resulting in one or more fruit of the Spirit. Christians were meant to be known as a united bunch of extravagant gift-givers. *"But the fruit of the Spirit is love, joy, peace, patience, kindness,*

---

13 Matthew 5:43-45.

goodness, faithfulness, gentleness, self-control; against such things there is no law." (Galatians 5:22-23). Gifts are given anytime. Fruit is gathered when it's mature and enjoyed when it's ripe. When your life begins radiating the fruit of the Spirit, gifts will follow. When you humbly deliver gifts of the Spirit, fruit will be the end result.

Pursue love. Humble yourself. Desire gifts. Bear fruit.

[Risk No. 291, 6/12/2013]
Hearing God on a Plane?

On one of many flights I had the privilege of sitting next to a sweet couple from Texas, where I was able to practice the gift of prophecy along with the gift of words of knowledge. We made small talk for a while and then I put on headphones and spent time with Jesus. I began sensing God giving me word-thoughts and prophetic insight for my neighbors. I wrote it all down. Sometimes it helps me to write down God-ideas for the sake of clarity and delivery. Here's what I wrote and shared with them:

I saw this couple as the kind of people who gave others space to be themselves. People felt they could be themselves because Derek and Robbi could be trusted. They were free-flowing and quick to bounce back. I saw them mentoring others—younger married couples—investing their time to help others especially in the area of clear communication. I also saw them wondering how to help the poor and needy and envisioned God bringing a sweet opportunity for them. Naturally generous. Jesus loves how they're wired and loves them like crazy. Neck/shoulder issues, especially in relation to sleeping awkwardly—needing pillows in all the right places. I saw Derek running and getting shin splints—problems from his knees down.

While I read the above out loud to them, they both were giving each other funny looks, like, How can this be? "So, wait, you just ask God and He speaks to you?"

"Yes, but I'm still learning to hear."

Robbi had only a few days prior considered a major job change to go back to school for counseling, specifically marriage and family. She was blown away. The neck/shoulder issues were spot on, even to the point of the pillows. Derek had endured five surgeries on his ankles for weak ankles and knees.

I held their hands and prayed over them. Robbi's neck and shoulders were instantly better and they were both freaking out. I reminded them how much Jesus loves them and knows them. Thank you, God.

[Risk No. 133, 02/18/2013]
Commanding Knees.

Colton reminded me of Mat Hoffman, the '90s BMX superstar. I asked Colton if he rode BMX bikes. He didn't. He *was* into motorcycles. I asked if Colton had ever crashed. He had. He had torn cartilage in both knees and broken his foot. I asked if there was still pain. There was, constantly, in both knees. "Colton, are you ready for this?" was the question zipping off my lips faster than I could catch it and push it back in. It wasn't an arrogant or prideful question, but my heart was full of faith that God would move. Sometimes this happens, and I feel the best description I can give is *the gift of faith for healing by the Spirit* comes over me and I just know God is going to do something amazing.

"Sure?" His response was timid. I held out my hand. Interesting how people will almost always stretch out their hands to take ours. Colton had no clue where I was heading when I began thanking Jesus for him, blessing his life and commanding his knees to be normal. I prayed and shared a word about how God wired him creative and a leader then asked him to check his knees. "This is really weird actually. They don't really hurt anymore. " Thank You, Jesus. My friend gave him a prophetic word regarding a relationship with a girl that God desired to reconcile. When asked if that made any sense, his response was encouraging. "Yeah, actually it does. That's really weird, too."

I asked Colton if he had a relationship with Jesus. "Well, no, I don't go to church. " Here in the pseudo-religious South we correlate going to church as personal relationship with Jesus. I rephrased; "Do you consider Jesus your best friend?" He did not. I asked Colton to do something that night before he went to bed. "Would you ask Jesus what it would look like to be his best friend?" I didn't feel I was to lead him in a prayer but rather lead him in a question that Jesus would gladly answer in His time.

[Risk No. 397, 09/17/2013]
One-Armed Painting.

A friend invited me out for coffee. We strolled into the narrow West Nashville coffee shop and were first in line. Two women came in right behind us. I thought I heard the word "painter" in my heart. As the ladies walked past our table on their way out, I took a messy risk. *"Are either of you painters, by chance?"* One pointed to the other, and they both looked at me, befuddled. Turns out they were mother and daughter and mother was the painter. "I am, but why do you ask?"

As I opened my mouth I found the Holy Spirit filling: "*I think you are discouraged and maybe about to give up on painting but God wants to remind you today that He's given you this gift and He's with you. Be encouraged.*" She was shocked and could hardly believe God would speak so clearly and obviously to her. My friend and I were able to pray over her struggling painting business. I then felt that she was having knee issues. I asked. She was. We prayed over her knees.

It was obvious that she was missing her right arm, so I asked what had happened. Cancer. "*I realize this might be the craziest offer you'll get all week, but can I pray Jesus grows your arm back?*" I mean, come on, why not pray the impossible? She smiled, shrugged, and said, "Go for it; that would be amazing. " We prayed restoration and commanded her arm to grow. The arm did not instantly reappear. I look forward to the day limbs do. Faith is certainty of what we don't see. Still, I was overjoyed by what God had already done. I praised Him for work accomplished and for what He would continue doing.

She hugged me and my heart ran full. As mother and daughter walked out, the mother turned to me and said, "I really needed that. " We all need reminders that God is far more clued-in than we even know. Gifts come wrapped.

[Risk No. 467, 11/05/2013]
Baptist Pastor and Local Tacos.

I met my pastor pal, Scott, at Local Taco. Scott works at a Baptist church in town and has a way of asking the best of questions. We shared a wonderful time. Earlier in the day, I had asked Jesus if there was anything He wanted to share with Scott through me. I received two *very* specific word-thoughts. I gave the usual prophetic waiver when I sense God has given me a specific word beyond a simple encouragement/reminder. This disclaimer helps set so many skeptic hearts at ease, including my own: "*First, I could be wrong. And, secondly, there's no pressure. If I'm wrong, please tell me so I can repent and ask God for greater grace in this area.*"

One of the prophetic words had to do with a resource project (come to find out Scott's working on a Bible translation resource) and the second was a personal issue pertaining to his wife. He was highly encouraged (as was I). One line he shared sticks with me still. "This was the first time I've received a word like this that *didn't* set me on guard. There was true humility in your delivery. Wow!" *Jesus, please help us only deliver what is rooted deep in humility. Guard us from pride.* Any delivery other than a humble one is a faux pas.

[Risk No. 622, 03/14/2014]
Problemas de Columna.

I knew I'd be meeting Milam for an early burrito lunch. During my routine "quiet time" (intentional space—early mornings in my world—for conversation with God) I envisioned a Hispanic woman behind the counter and heard the word, "columna. " I wasn't sure what columna translated to in English but figured if I saw a Hispanic lady at the register I'd ask. That's when I met Kristan.

I was able to speak to her in Spanish (grace!) and asked about her columna/espalda—spinal column/back—as I would soon find out. She was in pain and did have back/spinal column issues. We prayed over her and I encouraged her with how much God loves her. A few minutes later, I was up getting fiery salsa when she was filling the salsa bar. I asked how she felt. In Spanish: "Oh, I don't have any pain and I feel fine now!" *Jesus loves you. God bless you!*

There's something so special about the gift of words of knowledge, and all the gifts, of course, but the way in which God can cut through the awkward with a simple word of revelation about what an individual needs or desires is priceless. I want to grow more here, Jesus. Grow me. Grow us.

[Risk No. 623, 03/17/2014]
Awkward Times with a Plumber.

Plumber John has been to our house twice. The first time our dishwasher went out, and I did not offer to pray. The second time, I felt God was giving me a mind-picture of John and saw him as someone who might be an elder at a church. I asked him if the picture was true. Nope, at least not yet.

I then felt to ask him about any pain. Five years ago he had been in a car wreck and broken his hip/femur, and arthritis was setting in. I asked if I could pray. He awkwardly agreed. I commanded arthritis to flee and his body to be healed. Then I had the thought that maybe his right leg that had been broken was shorter than the left. I asked. It was. Without really thinking twice, I grabbed a chair and asked this six-foot-plus, fifty-year-old country man to take a seat in my dining room and to give me his legs. It was about as hilariously awkward as anything I've ever done.

"Leg: grow out in Jesus' name. Grow. Grow." I held them together—and where they once were off by a half inch or so—now both seemed perfectly aligned. I asked John to stand up and walk around. "Wow, that's weird. The catching isn't there anymore. Now I don't waddle like a penguin!" I reminded John how much Jesus loves and how much Jesus desires intimacy with him. Jesus.

Regardless of where you have or haven't been, one emphasis of this book is that God is still speaking, and not just to elite Christians, but to all of us. Learning to listen and discern *what* He's saying is one reason we're here together. Even when it doesn't seem so, the Christian life is supernatural to the core, including equally what we consider the modest *or* outlandish works of the Spirit.

Throughout these pages I have tried to provoke you toward growth in the "gifts" by way of stories that high-light "hearing from God" and stories that demonstrate my need to continue practicing. Each of us will progress and excel at a rate unique to who we are and to the gift (or gifts) the Spirit has given us. The point is that we hunger for Jesus, His righteousness and for increased momentum in developing spiritual gifts, no matter how long the journey takes us. Every Christian, including me, has ample room for growth in the empowerment God so generously offers.

10. Confessing Sin.

In a futile attempt to erase our past, we deprive the community of our healing gift. If we conceal our wounds out of fear and shame, our inner darkness can neither be illuminated nor become a light for others.

- Brennan Manning

Nothing spells defeat like unconfessed sin. I mentioned earlier the joys of flying buddy pass: pampered upgrades across the Atlantic with 180-degree flatbed seats, five-course meals, and vintage wine hand-picked by a master sommelier in Delta's business class. At the time of my earlier buddy pass story, I had never experienced the dark, disparaging downside. Yesterday rewired my perspective toward buddy passes. I arrived early in Fraport—Frankfurt, Germany's International airport—from a week of memorably special ministry at SMS, Steiger Missions School.

My time at Steiger International's headquarters—a former Nazi agricultural center in the wind turbine, electricity-converting, rolling farmlands of East Germany—represented one of the sweetest equipping experiences of my life. I witnessed powerful miracles of healing, prophetic insight and the joy of seeing old and new friends, including sixteen students from Ukraine whom I had met earlier in the year—nearly all had told me they would love to attend the school but couldn't afford it. God provides. Bonus to the miraculous, I met global youth from all over Europe, Brazil, New Zealand and beyond. These were no average college kids scouting for an easy summer break. I saw them and spotted their ache; a fiery hunger to see the kingdom of God displayed through naturally supernatural obedience.

Seated anxiously at the international airport gate, I forced back tears of hopeless frustration. The call came over terminal speakers that the second, and final, opportunity to catch a standby, return flight to America had come and gone. Never have I felt so alone and so far from family. Jesus calls us to make sacrifices—including being away from family—for the sake of the Gospel. Noble as that may sound now, I wouldn't be home as scheduled to hug my amazing kids or beautiful wife.

Under normal circumstances, being away for an extra day is hardly the end of the world. In this case, though, I was preparing to be home for only several short days before heading back out, this time to begin a ten-day, spiritually-heavy, film project on Middle Eastern youth living in Beirut, Lebanon. One day down meant even fewer days home.

I quickly booked a nearby hotel on Priceline, made arrangements to fly standby (all buddy pass flying is *standby* flying and not for the faint of heart like me) the following day, and dreaded the thought of informing my committed wife of 19 years that my family would have to manage another day without me. The family was seven hours behind me, and when I did talk to Beth at 6:19AM her time, she immediately asked, "Are you just messing with me or is this for real?"

It was real and, I fell hard as ever.

What I haven't told you yet is that I am a porn addict in recovery. Unlike my friends Tyler or Todd, I haven't experienced instant deliverance in this area, and I can't tell you this was *only* a problem of my pre-Christian past. Since the age of thirteen—when I was first exposed to a *Penthouse* magazine living tucked away on a tiny Caribbean island—I have struggled. You may feel it incomprehensible that this writer who claims to see Jesus often healing the sick is himself sometimes sick. And a good point you make. I have believed, and now continue believing, for the day when I can write a book about how I once battled lust-inspired demons. For now, I keep fighting, falling, repenting and praising God for grace greater than my sin-weakness.

While seated at gate D8 I wondered if there was some cosmic spiritual mystery as to why an entire flight—my flight—was cancelled on the only day I was trying to leave Germany. God knew my time with family was precious. He knew I would not take this news well. The redeeming factor, I clearly see now, is that, had I caught the original flight, I would never have included this chapter.

Maybe you—for sure me—needs to hear this. Rafael, a Steiger Missions School student told me a day prior how encouraged he was to discover I still wrestle with pornography. *Really? I'm not encouraged one bit.* He went on to say he was encouraged because apparently the Holy Spirit still moves powerfully through someone who struggles still. My weakness gave him hope. I pray this chapter, by far the hardest for me to write, provides you the same: hope.

The apostle Paul wrote—in every single letter—to the saints in every city he visited. He wrote to the saints at Ephesus, the saints at Corinth and the saints in Galatia. Even so, he dealt with problems of sin in the church. Pornography is what it is—miserable sin parading as graphic, intimate fulfillment. It's wrong, demeaning, self-serving and punches with the same addictive power as crack cocaine. Despite how sinful some of the early church members were (sleeping with a mother-in-law *or* getting drunk off communion elements are disturbing regardless of when in the time-frame of world they happened), Paul still wrote to saints. Why then is it so rare that we consider ourselves saints? Maybe because it's easier to allow Satan, accuser of the brethren, to convince us we're no better than our most recent failure than it is to believe that Jesus, in all His glory, lives to make intercession for messy us. He purchased our purity, even when we stumble and slip backward. I don't for a second condone sin nor hold to the idea of "cheap grace" that claims you can do whatever you want without regards to being holy as He is holy. [14] Jesus considers each of His follower's saints who, on occasion, fall to sin in varying degrees. God sees us for the work His Son accomplished on the cross. When we surrender to that great work, the blood washes over us. Clean. I am a saint who sometimes sins, not a sinner who sometimes saints.

While frustrated and waiting for the next flight out of Germany, I regretfully binged on porn for many false-pleasure hours in a dim, empty hotel room. Alone—embarrassing and shameful—but painfully real. The arrangement Beth and I have had for years is that *if* I have looked at porn, I must confess to Jesus, several of my brothers, and be transparent with her. Not only did I make it home a day late, but I broke the human heart that matters most to mine. Again.

So, why in the world am I telling you this and what connection does any of it have with taking risks? When I fall into sin that goes unconfessed for any length of time, it becomes near impossible to love neighbors as I am loved. I interacted with at least ten people en route back home. I didn't even offer to pray for a single one of them. No prophetic words. I saw several sick or hurting people and passed them all by. This is the power of unconfessed sin—where my heart has no room for carrying love—a tomb for shame, guilt, and heaviness. Yes, I confessed my sin to Jesus and, unbelievably, He again forgave me. But when sin involves someone else—in this case a direct offense against Beth and the brothers I'm accountable to—confession doesn't end with Jesus. Confession starts with Him and ends with whoever I've directly offended. *"Confess your sins to one another that you may be healed. The prayer of the righteous man (he who is in right standing with God) is powerful and effective."*

---

14 1 Peter 1:16, reference.

(James 5:16, paraphrased).

Most of the stories I included in this chapter have little to do with confession of sin. I included them because it's important for you to see what God can do when we're living free. None of these accounts would have been possible had I been weighed down by guilt or buried in shame and condemnation. *"There is therefore now no condemnation for those who are in Christ Jesus."* (Romans 8:1).

During a speaking workshop at the Steiger International base, I shared how my friend Aaron and I were walking through JFK airport routing back from Kiev via Moscow when I noticed a cruel sight. A teenage boy seemed to possess a square beard that hung four inches below his face. Except this was no hipster beard. Somehow in my heart I knew it was a tumor. The tumor had been growing in this boy's lower face, majorly distorting the skin around his neck, cheeks and lower lip. I looked at Aaron and acted quickly. We high speed shuffled over to the young man who was about to exit out the airport doors.

Our interruption revealed his parents as the couple walking behind him. They were from Switzerland visiting the U. S. for a highly specialized surgical removal. I shared how God had given me compassion for healing and asked if we could pray for their son. They kindly agreed. We prayed the surgery would be successful and that the tumor would be completely removed. The boy's parents thanked us for our care and encouragement, especially receiving this level of affection on their first time visiting the States before even having walked out of the airport. We hugged and continued on our way.

While sharing this story (which I had not even planned on sharing) at the Steiger school, I noticed big tears welling up in Anya's eyes. We had talked earlier and I recalled her being from Switzerland. Her tears were enough for me to recognize that she knew this boy. I quickly found myself asking, *"You know this boy?"* She nodded. The entire class (including me) stood stunned silent. Anya had been working in a children's hospital until quitting to attend the ten-week training school. She had worked with this boy many times and had always *wished* she could pray for him, something which was not legal apart from a patient's request.

The last time she had seen the boy was just before his departure to the U. S. for the intensive surgery. She could hardly believe Aaron and I had met him in the airport. I stood stunned a little while longer, trying to process. What were the odds? *Out of seventy students on a missions base in the middle of nowhere Germany, one would have prayed a prayer that God may have answered through us.* Following the Holy Spirit into spontaneous storytelling brings about results only God could deliver. Not only was Anya from Switzerland, but she actually had cared for the only person from Switzerland I've ever prayed for in public. Neither Anya nor I know whether the surgery was successful or whether the boy was supernaturally healed. The point God was making to me was that He knows everything and has no trouble connecting dots in such a way that is otherwise inexplicable by my finite understanding.

[Risk No. 106, 02/05/2013]
Headaches and My Fear.

During a mid-morning prayer meeting, I prayed for a friend's wife who I had never met before. While praying for her, I kept sensing the word "headache." I quietly confessed being afraid to ask in front of everyone, but as prayer ended, I still wasn't able to get the idea out of my heart.

I finally approached her. *"Hey, Sarah, do you deal with headaches, especially from tension in your neck?"* Her husband instantly confirmed,

CHAD JOHNSON

me) stood stunned silent. Anya had been working in a children's hospital until quitting to attend the ten-week training school. She had worked with this boy many times and had always *wished* she could pray for him, something which was not legal apart from a patient's request.

The last time she had seen the boy was just before his departure to the U. S. for the intensive surgery. She could hardly believe Aaron and I had met him in the airport. I stood stunned a little while longer, trying to process. What were the odds? *Out of seventy students on a missions base in the middle of nowhere Germany, one would have prayed a prayer that God may have answered through us.* Following the Holy Spirit into spontaneous storytelling brings about results only God could deliver. Not only was Anya from Switzerland, but she actually had cared for the only person from Switzerland I've ever prayed for in public. Neither Anya nor I know whether the surgery was successful or whether the boy was supernaturally healed. The point God was making to me was that He knows everything and has no trouble connecting dots in such a way that is otherwise inexplicable by my finite understanding.

[Risk No. 106, 02/05/2013]
Headaches and My Fear.

During a mid-morning prayer meeting, I prayed for a friend's wife who I had never met before. While praying for her, I kept sensing the word "headache." I quietly confessed being afraid to ask in front of everyone, but as prayer ended, I still wasn't able to get the idea out of my heart.

I finally approached her. *"Hey, Sarah, do you deal with headaches, especially from tension in your neck?"* Her husband instantly confirmed,

98

and I instantly praised God. For two years Sarah had dealt with headaches due to tension/stress in her neck. I told her how God sometimes gives me insight over others because He desires to heal them. She wasn't currently experiencing a headache, but we prayed, rebuking stress, pain, and tension. I was able to encourage her with words God gave me specific to how He sees her. Sometimes your risk is being willing to share what comes to heart even after you've confessed fear.

God, You are incredible. I am awed by You. Help us never stop risking in this messy, extravagant new. I confess how often I'm afraid, how often I give my ears to fear.

If you deal with headaches, migraines, head trauma, brain diseases/disorders, memory loss of any kind, attention deficit issues, brain tumors, etc:. *In Jesus' name, be made whole. Pain and problems: leave now and never return.*

[Risks No. 427, 10/04/2013]
Hot Dogs: Window to the Soul?

Stephanie was working at The Dog, David's favorite post-soccer practice stop. I shared with Stephanie how I felt God saw her. "*I see you as the kind of person that looks forward to the next challenge. You see possible when others see impossible.*"

She was puzzled. "Wait, who did you say told you that?"

"*God did. Does it make any sense to you?*"

"Yeah, totally!" *Awesome, God loves you!*

Prophetic words don't have to be complicated to be profound.

One week later, David wanted The Dog—again. Guess who smiled at us. "I remember you!"

"*We remember you too!*"

I asked how Stephanie was doing and told her the last time I had been in, my back had been hurting, and I wondered if she dealt with any back issues. "No, not back issues. "

"*Pain anywhere else?*"

"Not pain, but I've been dealing with nightmares for four years, and I don't sleep well as a result. "

"*Oh wow, I was way off but can I pray Jesus helps you anyway?*"

"Yes, that would be great. " I asked for her hand and from across the counter commanded nightmares to end and true peace to begin.

While David and I were eating I couldn't help but think that Stephanie did not know Jesus. Before we left I asked if she considered Jesus her best friend. "No, not really. "

"*Well, I think He's about to become your best friend. I encourage you to ask Him to be your friend and to start showing you what that looks like. The reason these different things have happened is purely because Jesus thinks you're amazing and loves you like crazy.*"

Her smile spelled, "this is so weird but so right. " She thanked me profusely for caring. I didn't sense I was to lead her to Jesus on the spot, though I'm confident I could have. Instead, I felt God prompted me to pray close Christian friends around her would rise to the occasion. On the way home, David said, "Dad, I feel like we should ask God to help her become a Christian before this year is over." We prayed just that.

I caved—again—when David (with his sister chiming in this time) begged for a post-soccer trip to The Dog. And, again, who was at the counter greeting us? None other than our sweet Stephanie. I asked how her nightmares had been since we prayed several weeks back. "They're gone! I am so glad to see you. I can't believe what's been happening. I don't even know how to thank you!" Since the last time we had seen her, Stephanie attended church for the first time with the one roommate who "loves God." She was shining and I was able to pray for her again and continued investing in her. If Stephanie was the only fruit that came from my messy, extravagant risks, she's well worth it.

When I first began to stretch my prophetic wings, I made many a mistake (which, as much as I'd like to tell you I've arrived at perfect hearing, and sharing, that is far from the case). One of the more notable "misses" was with my friends in the band *Sleeping Giant*. We were on a mini-tour in 2007 or 2008 with a stop in Albuquerque, New Mexico. During a pre-show prayer time in the makeshift green room (a space that serves as a waiting room/lounge for performers before and after their public appearance), my attention was drawn to Eric, *Sleeping Giant's* guitar player. Anyone who knows Eric will know his tattooed, pierced, often serious exterior is only a cover for joy-filled sensitivity. Eric, a pastor, successful businessman, video producer, and gifted creative is also one of the most sensitive—to the Holy Spirit—people I know.

Eric was sitting away from everyone else in the backstage office, working away on his laptop. I sensed—and publicly shared—two things about him. One, that he was dealing with depression. Two, that he was struggling with an addiction to pornography.

Years later, the memory of this "prophetic moment" came back to me. I sensed the Holy Spirit asking me, "Do you remember that time you 'prophesied' over Eric?" I unfortunately did. "Well, you were totally off. Eric doesn't deal with either of those things, and you were not hearing from Me." Ouch. I did the only rational thing I knew to do. Apologize. First, to the Holy Spirit. Second, I called Eric. I had hoped he would have forgotten the whole ordeal, sparing me the awkward confession. If you've spent any time in the charismatic Christian world—especially in the prophetic context—you'll often hear people pray a disclaimer like, "Lord, if any of this is not from You, please allow them to not remember any of it—like water cascading off a duck's back. . . .".

From the other end of the phone (which, shockingly, Eric still answered when I called) came the straightforward response I had not hoped for. "Yeah man, I remember that." I further explained what I felt the Holy Spirit had just told me. Eric kindly responded: "Yep, that's true what the Holy Spirit just told you, I don't deal with either of those issues." Eric thanked me for owning up to my mistake and for apologizing. I thanked him for being a gracious friend to me and grew immensely through the whole messy debacle.

Looking back, the reason I sensed depression was likely because I paid more attention to his demeanor than any kind of Holy Spirit prompting. And the pornography thought was probably my own addiction transposed onto him. Either way, Eric and the other members of *Sleeping Giant* were beyond gracious to this newbie practicing spiritual gifts, who at the very least, ought to have privately approached Eric asking if either of the thoughts I was perceiving applied to him.

Confess sin often and regularly—to God and neighbors. Jesus will be honored, and humility will become a strong shield about you.

11. Rejected; but Oh, So Loved!

More than that, we rejoice in our sufferings, knowing that suffering produces endurance, and endurance produces character, and character produces hope, and hope does not put us to shame, because God's love has been poured into our hearts through the Holy Spirit who has been given to us.

- Romans 5:3-5

When we risk, and are rejected, fear, insecurity, and intimidation blend and are then thrown. No one likes rejection. Fewer welcome it. Jesus was rejected and promised His followers they could anticipate the same. *"If the world hates you, know that it has hated me before it hated you."* (John 15:18). To develop a life of risk isn't to ignore rejection when it does show up; it is to taste—even for a slight moment—the highest price of treasuring Jesus. *"The one who hears you hears me, and the one who rejects you rejects me, and the one who rejects me rejects him who sent me."* (Luke 10:16). Jesus was rejected in his own hometown. He was rejected in Jerusalem. I can only assume He disliked rejection as much as you or I. Never did He shy away from rejection, though, even proving on the cross that His heart was pure and unoffended. The experience of rejection, whenever it comes (and if you follow Jesus, it will come), is a reminder to love *regardless* of the response. Take a risk, your Father is king over *unremarkable old* rejection.

Rejection from family members or close friends usually hurts most, but even rejection from strangers in foreign lands can carry a sting.

Turkey is an increasingly unstable Middle Eastern country confronted by growing challenges. Syrian refugees fleeing ISIS, thirty-year feuds with a Kurdish rebel group, and most recently 14 suicide bombings since June of 2014. [15] The phrase "To be a Turk is to be Muslim and to be Muslim is to be a Turk" illustrates the centuries-old, deep-seeded roots of Turkey's 80-million-member population. Turkey is made up of an estimated 99.8%[16] Muslims, with only 4,500[17] professing Christians—making it the largest unreached nation on the planet—and a country I expected to experience a great deal of rejection in.

Artists on mission, like *No Longer Music (NLM)*, face rejection consistently. For thirty years *NLM* have been touring faraway and far-out places proclaiming the love of Jesus—free of charge and always as "musicianaries" on mission facing rejection more consistently than any other artist I've partnered with. They're as radical as anyone I've met. If you've never heard of *No Longer Music*, think *Blue Man Group* theatrics meets choreographed dance-pop meets *Rob Zombie* pyrotechnics meets *Billy Graham* preaching. I know, it's weird. Even weirder in a Middle Eastern culture with no frame of reference for anything of the sort. But they communicate with passion and effect.

The stories in this chapter pertain to rejection, or at least the threat thereof. Each story was taken from Middle Eastern experiences I've had with the bands *No Longer Music* and *Alegorica* who are both *Come&Live!* artists living to proclaim and demonstrate the gospel of Jesus outside of the church.

---

15 https://www.nytimes.com/2016/06/29/travel/is-istanbul-safe-what-travelers-should-know.html

16 https://en.wikipedia.org/wiki/Islam_in_Turkey

17 https://en.wikipedia.org/wiki/Protestantism_in_Turkey

[Risk No. 780, 8/29/2014]
The Only Time Someone Offered to Remove My Head From My Body.

Our night together in Manavgat (which in Turkish sounds strangely like "man-of-God") was by far the most peculiar and powerful, while on tour in Turkey. The evening began quite different for our friends in *No Longer Music* in contrast to any other night on their five-month-long international tour. For starters, they hadn't been invited and didn't have official permission (whereas all the other performances came by invitation and permission). Secondly, there was no electricity, so their usual high energy audio/visual set was stripped down to a minimal drums and skit vibe. They played two shows back to back. Hundreds gathered impromptu for each.

Halfway through the first performance, I noticed a man in the crowd making gestures at us. Apparently this man didn't appreciate us, our message, or both—which I wisely deduced from fingers slid slowly across his throat followed by a firm pointing in our direction. Not knowing what else to do, I began praying in the Spirit (another way of saying I was hyperventilating in tongues). I had no clue what this man was yelling other than something along the lines of "Allahu Akbar! (Allah is Greater)!" This man even approached our interpreter, Şafak, trying to shut him up. Surprisingly, Şafak shoved him away and pushed through. Throat-slitting pointer man returned to where he previously stood, clearly stirring the crowd against us.

After *NLM's* first set, I approached a group of people and asked if anyone was in pain. My new friend, Benjamin, kindly translated for me on the spot and informed me one of the young guys had a knee problem. We prayed, and pain was instantly gone. The young man and I began jogging to test the prayer and his body. His knee felt 100% better. Just prior to this I noticed some of the *NLM* crew in heated debate with several Turkish men. I had recognized one as the man who angrily shouted, threatened, and pointed—especially while David was sharing about Jesus.

I returned from jogging with the boy whose knee had just been healed, turned to my left, and found "throat-slitting-gesture-guy" standing literally right in front of me—*way* too close for comfort. In what seemed like a split second, I asked the Spirit for help. What I sensed—in equally split second—was that I should *hug* him. My options were limited, so I went with embracing "threatening man" and hoped to Heaven he would return the offer. It was one of those moments where time stood still. I thought it would be mechanically harder for this man to cut my head off with my arms wrapped around his back. I breathed many sighs of relief when he responded by throwing his arms tightly around me, and we embraced, for a time much longer than Westerners know to appreciate. In this situation, awkward hugging was far more my speed than head removal.

What I had not realized was that head-cutting, awkward-hugger had been watching as God touched the young man's knee. Suat, as he introduced himself to me, began showing me all the areas he had pain or physical problems. He lifted up the back of his shirt to reveal a scar on his lower right side. He then grabbed my right hand and applied it to his scar, motioning with his hands (interpreter Benjamin had long disappeared at this point) for me to do that thing I did for the knee. We prayed. Same drill, Suat with shirt pulled up to reveal stab wound on the left side of his chest, instructed me to pray. A third and final time, he requested I pray for an indentation on his skull accompanied by what must have been thirty staples from a former accident. I began realizing why this man would have threatened us—he was clearly hurting. With the Father, Son, and Holy Spirit, you are never alone.

After a sweet time of prayer over each of these issues, Suat suggested, again with his hands, that I should buy him a drink. I agreed. We walked a few feet from the main square into a market, and he asked for beer. I tried explaining how beer is about 95% water and therefore we should stick with water. Though he couldn't understand me, he seemed OK with my reasoning.

The man behind the cashier was blind in his right eye. Before I knew what was happening, Suat took hold of my right hand and stretched it across the counter, placing it directly over this unsuspecting man's eye. Suat again insinuated I should do that thing I do. Pray. I commanded blindness to leave. No obvious change was discernible, but language proved my barrier as I wasn't able to ask whether anything was happening. Lord, help us trust You to move even when we have no clue. The man behind the market register seemed grateful enough.

As we walked outside, drinking purified bottled water, Suat insinuated we should hold tight right where we were. I stood stunned, unsure of what he meant. I watched as he went out into the crowd. Much to my surprise, Suat returned with a handful of needy people. Around this time he also began calling me "Papa", which apparently means *pope* in Turkish. I'm far from the Pope, but it is amazing that Christ calls us all *ambassadors*. Suat first brought us a young woman who seemed a likely crack addict (judging purely by her rotting teeth and dilated pupils). Though we didn't understand each other's words, I held her hands and began blessing her life, inviting Jesus to touch down and move in power. Her smile was like stepping into another world. She came alive, giggling to the funny sound of my English praying. Her whole face radiated two things: "Someone noticed me, for me. Someone is loving me, for me."

Halil was next to be brought our way (by now a prayer line had formed thanks to Suat). Several of my *No Longer Music* friends were with me during this time. Suat strongly suggested, demanded may have been more accurate, that we pray for Halil's ears. Though we had no clue what was wrong, we began praying. Then it was his left wrist. As we prayed, his eyes widened. He smiled. Huge. We knew Jesus was present.

I was clueless, but somewhere Suat had found six teenagers on motorcycles that he insisted required prayer. The only man who has ever threatened to sever my head from my body was now recruiting unsuspecting passersby for prayer. One of these spoke a little English so we asked about pain and began praying. Once again: Jesus. I gathered as many of the teenagers as were willing to circle up and hold hands, praying Jesus would draw each of them into His presence. Joy to the brim.

By this time, NLM had begun their second performance and hundreds more had gathered to watch the odd spectacle. Instead of the loud insurgent that Suat once represented, he was now boasting a new job description. He was walking through the crowd, telling anyone who was talking to be silent and to pay attention to the show. He would stand next to me, pinch his shirt as to imply he was wearing a suit and tie, and in serious form would look me in the eyes. He would say, "Security. Security!" I clearly understood what he meant. Suat was my bodyguard. From threat to prayer team volunteer to protector. He was additionally encouraging others to give us their contact information so they could learn more about Jesus. It was bizarre. Suat was a different man, and I was living a dream. Whatever threat once possessed him had long departed.

We prayed for several others once the second concert ended, but I focused my energy on Halil as I felt Jesus making this clear to me. Halil had grown up as a traditional Muslim who had adopted atheism as his belief stance—as did many youth we met. David, a faithful long-term missionary from Iowa serving tirelessly in the Middle East, helped me communicate the Gospel in Turkish to Halil. Halil's wrist had been completely healed when we had prayed for it earlier, and we discovered he was dealing with sinus issues affecting his eyes, head, and ears. We prayed again and instructed Halil to try taking two deep breaths through his nose. On his first attempt at nasal breathing, he nearly fell over. It was the first time in a long time he was able to breathe properly. His face spelled wonder. Minutes later, Halil asked Jesus to become his best friend and savior.

Suat was now sitting on a bench quietly waiting for us as we wrapped up prayer times and conversations with others. I knew he was next when I learned it was time for us to leave. I wrestled with what to do. I sensed the Holy Spirit say, "Go to him!" As quickly as I asked if he wanted to experience the same love we carried from Jesus, the only Son of God, he nodded in thrilled agreement. Unreal. The Muslim man who had only two hours earlier threatened to cut our heads off or shoot us was now surrendering himself to Jesus. Take a messy, extravagant risk; your Father is King of the Universe.

My heart melted for Suat. He struck me as the kind of man desperate for attention, hungry for a touch. Jesus gave us grace to be His hands and feet in the face of rejection. Before we turned to walk away, Şafak offered Suat his flip-flops as it was obvious Suat's flip-flops had seen better days. The flip-flops didn't fit, and I offered mine only to discover the same problem. Marcel, from Brazil, was playing bass in *NLM* and had been with me for most of the evening. He offered his new Vans to Suat, and they fit perfectly. I'm not sure I've ever seen a man more joyously excited. Jesus had entered his life, and he was experiencing the first touch of adoption into this incredible Kingdom family. God is all-powerful, and He is drawing all men unto Himself.

Would you pour out more of Your Spirit on Turkey, Lord? That Turkey, and all of the Middle East, would embrace you, not only as prophet, but as King and friend.

Before venturing into Lebanon, my second exposure to the Middle East, I asked my missionary-friend Lukas (who relocated his family from the comforts of Switzerland to serve full-time in Beirut) if he was aware of any Jesus stories we should consider capturing. We were introduced to many in the Middle East who had come to Jesus in radical, profound ways. No two stories were the same. Each was as unique as the person we talked to. We met former Muslims who had turned from Islam embracing everything from atheism to mysticism to Satanism before following Jesus. We heard of God flowing through dreams, visions, supernatural visitations, physical healing, His followers, and in one case, through simply reading the Qur'an and the Bible side by side. I quickly discovered Jesus spared no expense to reach the least of these. He *so* loved the world that He gave Himself for *all* of us.

Music happened to be the tool God used in outfitting the men and women I was with. They came from all over the world in an effort to share good news with peers of equally diverse backgrounds. *Alegorica* is from Brazil, of all unlikely places far removed from the Middle East. They came to Beirut unsure of what to expect, but committed to the trip regardless of whether a single show was confirmed. *Alegorica* and I shared many Spirit-inspired moments with lovely people as we went about setting up, performing, tearing down, or just walking through a mall. If you're willing to carry love wherever you go, fruit will naturally spill over. Raymonda was one such extravagant spill.

Alegorica was scheduled to perform their set at an art gallery in the historic club district of Beirut. Several minutes into their set, the show was abruptly shut down by local authorities claiming violation of a noise ordinance. Rejection, though not on the grounds of faith. The band desperately wanted to finish their set. Beirut police felt audibly otherwise. *Alegorica* decided to close the night by gathering the small crowd into a circle to share *why* they were in Beirut. By the end of our awkward, impromptu conversation in the art gallery, I sensed the Holy Spirit giving me several word-thoughts for people dealing with physical problems. I asked if anyone sensed a connection to my word-thoughts. At first everyone just looked at me like I was crazy. Rejection, light. Then, after several awkward moments, our new friend, and art gallery manager, Raymonda, shared how every symptom I just mentioned applied perfectly to her.

We prayed and simultaneously watched Jesus heal Raymonda. She repeatedly exclaimed how weird and different she was feeling. I asked if she had ever met Jesus as her best friend. She hadn't, though she had grown up nominally Christian. At first, she seemed an odd combination of skeptical and puzzled. I challenged her with what she had to lose. If Jesus is who He says He is, He would turn her world upside down. If He isn't the Son of God, what could possibly go wrong? She agreed to pray a simple prayer inviting Jesus to reveal Himself to her. Raymonda then asked me an honest question regarding God's ability to help in the area of a serious issue she was struggling through. "Of course He can help!," slipped out of my mouth before I even had time to consider what I was saying. I prayed a ludicrous prayer, inviting the Holy Spirit to show me Raymonda's secret struggle. Seconds later, I sensed a mental picture of a toy firecracker—the kind of party favor (or Christmas cracker) that pops as you pull on both ends. I shared the picture and found the Holy Spirit giving me greater understanding. In my mind, I saw Raymonda as the firecracker, with two hands pulling either side. Each hand represented a different man. Her expression spelled severe shock, though she didn't feel comfortable telling me what was going on. We invited Raymonda to hang out with us the very next evening, at a different club for another

Alegorica performance. She showed up together with a man. I ended up praying and talking with other people after the show, but I did notice my friends interviewing Raymonda and the man who had joined her. On the drive home my friends were like animated sparks, "Dude! Do you know who that was? That was her husband! Apparently at the show last night she was deciding whether or not she should leave her husband for another man!" Unbeknownst to me, she had indeed brought her estranged husband—one of the two hands I had seen in my mind-picture the night prior.

Upon hearing this, I hoped and prayed God would make a way for me to spend time with the reunited couple. They agreed to meet with me on my final night in Lebanon. Hours before I caught a midnight flight out of Beirut, I found myself sitting outside talking, encouraging, and praying over this couple. Raymonda shared how only three days prior, before meeting us, she had planned to leave her husband for another man. After meeting us—and encountering Jesus—she had a heart change. She had begun sensing a profoundly renewed love for her husband. Her husband, Ghaith, was raised Muslim but walked away from Islam, turning instead to Satan worship. He rolled up his pant leg revealing a tattoo illustrating his former life—pentagram and all. Ghaith began sharing his thoughts on Jesus and *four* different ways in which Jesus had revealed himself. Instead of trying to cleverly polish and retell his words, I feel the Holy Spirit leading me to allow Ghaith to speak for himself, word for word, and tell you directly.

Jesus was always there for me. I used to always encounter Him, in a way. But I didn't accept the way that Jesus dealt with me. I grew up being a wolf, fighting for my rights. On the streets there is no such thing as mercy. I wasn't convinced that I loved Him as a person for the things He'd done. I loved the story, but I wasn't convinced. I didn't understand the whole cheek thing. Because you can't turn your cheek. If you turned one, you get another one - and you'd get beat on...

Encounter one. *But Jesus once came to my dream. It was a face, like I don't know, I don't know how to describe it. His face was so beautiful. I don't know how to describe it. It's weird. You can't describe it. It was very beautiful. He's so beautiful.... I didn't see a light like around his head, but his beauty—his face—is light. I don't know how to tell you. It's very hard to describe. His face is like a shining face. She (Raymonda) knows I love Jesus a lot. I love Him. I respect Him a lot you know? Because this was how I was raised. You respect Him first. It's all about respect. So I respected Him a lot. I respected what He did. And I was talking to Raymonda about Him and then his face again came to me. I couldn't help it but I felt like crying. Even so, I wasn't crying. I don't cry a lot. But He was there. The emotions were there and His face was there.*

Encounter two. *I was driving. But the picture was blank, time stopped. Maybe I was talking honestly about him, about my love for Him. As a person, as a guy. Not just as a prophet, as a person. So I saw His face again and I felt Him this time. I wasn't dreaming, I was driving. And I was with Raymonda. I held it in because I didn't want to have her see me crying. But I was holding back tears and beginning to choke. That was the second time.*

Encounter three. *Once I was meditating. This happened a few months ago. And I was wondering...I was lonely actually. I was feeling really lonely. In the deep meditation, Jesus came to me and just held my hand. It was like He was walking with me. But I'm not alone. I was in deep, deep meditation. So I smiled and said "can I know You more?" Like the feeling of being more with me. I'm real; I'm being real. You know you have no one in life. You sit in your room coming from work, and every night is the same. I don't do TV, I don't do nothing. Just with yourself, you don't have no one. You feel lonely. You always feel lonely after a while. Especially because we (he and Raymonda) weren't together then. So you feel lonely, and then Jesus came to me and said you're not alone. I said, "Ok, Yes - thank You. Can we do it again, please?" It was a very, very nice feeling. Just the image of Him holding my hand, it's like I'm His son and He's walking with me always.*

Encounter four. The fourth time I met Jesus, I encountered Jesus, it was yesterday when I saw her with you. But this time I didn't see the vision, this time I saw the action of Jesus. Because I know this is an act of Jesus. You don't have to see his face or to feel these powerful emotions every time. Jesus is telling me "I'm here and look what I'm doing." Yeah, I consider this the fourth time I encountered Jesus, and I'm still encountering Him right now. For me it's not to live pain-free, because it's not. For me to have the pain, to accept the pain, to trust that it's OK. That it will be OK, to trust God and His path for you.

For me to know God is not something easy because Raymonda knows that I didn't like life. I tried suicide so many times in my life. And the marks are still here. The last time I threw myself into the sea, but I didn't die. One time I had a gun in my mouth, but I couldn't pull the trigger. But she knows that for me, I'm not that good in life. But I'll always give God another chance to represent Himself—to be with us. I'm praying because I'm experiencing something. Not something that someone told me or something they explained. I've been through all this shit, and I found God. How do you think someone became a saint? Who became the first saint? The first saint was Jesus. It was like a father carrying me along like I was his son…Jesus, we surrender our hearts. . .

With barely two hours to spare before our flight departure, this struggling couple agreed to invite Jesus into their hearts—and marriage. The *unremarkable old* made *messy extravagant new.* Jesus loves the world so much that He'll send you to places like Beirut simply to remind lonely sons and conflicted daughters that He's present.

This final story on rejection took place on my third trip to the Middle East, this time back to Turkey and it illustrates how God seems to have a knack for saving the best for last. It was the second to last day of the tour and that afternoon, during our group prayer time, I confessed feeling discouraged. I had no desire for being there, and I had no hope.

Izmir, Turkey, is the city where Syrian refugees had congregated by the thousands in hopes of a new, better life just across the Aegean Sea to Greece and onward to the European Union. *No Longer Music* was performing two separate sets, sharing the Gospel with hundreds of youth. At one point during their second set, I noticed a group of young men waving a Turkish flag, wearing political party bandanas, chanting something in Turkish. They turned the corner toward us and stood disruptively cheering—drawing attention away from David's preaching—rejecting whatever he was saying for whatever it was they were chanting.

The show had just about ended while our friends tried settling the issue these men had against us. Seconds after the performance, I asked David for the microphone and shared several word-thoughts I sensed the Holy Spirit laying on my heart for those hurting. I invited anyone who needed prayer to come over to the side. It was dark, and at the time I didn't realize the man seated in the grass closest to me was the leader of the group chanting against us. Jesus was wonderfully healing and restoring many when our interpreter, Şafak, called me over to pray with this same man.

I asked how I could pray, and Coşkun (pronounced Josh-koon) responded by saying his life was empty and horrible, but that he sensed joy in us. Coşkun asked how he could have what we had. If that wasn't a setup for salvation, I'm not sure what is. Şafak, our interpreter friend, is Kurdish. Coşkun was demonstrating for a racist, anti-Kurdish, nationalist government party, what we might compare to a white supremacist leading a small KKK rally. Şafak and I shared the Gospel with a man whose given name translates to exuberant, fiery *and* joyful. What "Joyful" wanted most from us was joy. We dropped to our knees together with him, and prayed Coşkun would begin following Jesus and growing with Him all the days of his life. We knelt down right there, and in a swift instant, leader of the troublemakers handed his heart to Jesus. It seems that when I'm feeling least spiritual, or least prepared, Jesus shows up in amazing ways that further demonstrate it's not about me. We bought Coşkun a meal, spent time encouraging him, as well as connected him with local pastors.

Rejection, whether in the form of light prayer turn-downs or threats of a head severed from the body, or anything in between, are opportunities for our faith, hope and love to be stretched. If we're to grow in this area of developing a life of risk, rejection will find us sooner than later. The grace of God is powerful enough to move you through it.

Jesus, teach us to embrace rejection and help us never to reject others regardless of whether they've rejected us.

12. Right Place, Right Time.

Humble yourselves, therefore, under the mighty hand of God so that at the proper time he may exalt you, casting all your anxieties on him, because he cares for you...

- 1 Peter 5:6&7

Impressing my kids was easy after meeting a real-life orc.

While sipping a flat white in Auckland, New Zealand, I felt I recognized a man walking by. Excusing myself from the group, I walked up to this tall Kiwi and asked if he knew any of my Kiwi friends. I was wrong; he didn't. No matter, a conversation with a stranger is one step closer to conversation with a friend. Clinton and I began talking when I soon felt Jesus giving me words of encouragement for him. I asked if I could share the words and pray over him. We prayed together, and I asked more about his story. He asked if I wanted to know a fun fact. Of course I did. Facts are rarely fun in my mind, but Clinton changed all that. Turns out my new friend had played one of the lead Uruk-hai roles in all three *Lord of the Rings* movies. Crazy. Prophetic words and prayer times for one of Sauron's orcs. What J. R. R. Tolkien dreamt, I met. Underneath all that grime, blood and matted hair was a person pursued and loved by the King of the Universe.

You can start risking by flashing a stranger a smile. Yes, even smiles may feel awkward at first, but they're still so fundamental. Give of yourself a little more generously to someone around you. Add an extra zero to the tip on your next eating-out meal. Ask the homeless person standing outside the store if they need anything while you're inside the store. Buy and give. On your next trip to Crema's Coffee, Intelligentsia, Stumptown or wherever you sip espresso, offer to return to your co-worker with a latte—for them. No plant grows without someone first sowing a seed.

Frequently, we associate generosity with our money, or at least the times we give our money, and this is a valid, valuable part of developing a life of risk. Generosity also comes in the less-often-considered form of our time, and how willing we are to share it. You and I never know how far God might take any one of our individual encounters until after we've lived the story, so being flexible with our time is a beautiful offering in the messy, extravagant new. Making ourselves available to the Holy Spirit is the best way to offer our hearts and our time to the One who is most capable of positioning us perfectly when and where. Timing was critically crucial to each of the stories I've included in this chapter, none of which I anticipated or planned. I pray they help remind you that leaving time in God's hands is better than any amount of stressing or worrying we could produce ourselves.

[Risk No. 125, 02/13/2013]
Perfect Timing and Secret Powers.

I noticed a tall man with sweet dreads walking away from the "quick" oil-change station I had just pulled into. So much in American life continues to move toward instant fulfillment, the oil replaced in my car is no exception. The word-thought "ankle" came to my heart the second I saw the tall, dreaded man. I offered my keys and took a seat in the back of the waiting room. Within a matter of minutes, my name was called. I was somewhat surprised to realize LaMont was who I had seen earlier. We talked about the weather and how LaMont loves Miami, especially for the topless beaches. He asked me how much I'd love to be at a topless beach. Tempting, especially for a recovering lust addict, but I shared how I'm happily married and how Jesus has been healing me of fleshly desires. His countenance instantly shifted. I didn't bash him, just shared how I didn't need a topless beach to satisfy my deepest longings. Jesus is enough, He really is.

I asked if either ankle was giving him trouble. "Yeah, my right one." Turns out he was born with flat arches, and over the past few years, the right ankle has been a major problem. He's been to doctors, worn boots, braces, and taken all kinds of meds. None of it worked. I asked for LaMont's hand. He freely offered it. With his hand in mine, I rebuked pain and commanded his foot to work again. *"LaMont, try walking around on it a bit and tell me how it feels."* He walked outside into the oil changing space.

Within a couple minutes he returned with a quizzical look asking me, "Do you have some kind of secret power?" *"I do, but He's no secret. His name is Jesus. He made you, He loves you, and He has a plan for your life."* LaMont continued to express how strange this was. We prayed a second time that the little remaining pain would leave. He walked outside a second time.

Enter Kevin. Kevin was one of LaMont's co-workers. I asked if Kevin had any back problems. He used to but was fine now, causing me to wonder if I ask about back problems more than any other issue because of how often I've seen backs healed. I asked if he had pain anywhere else. "My teeth are killing me because I just had all four wisdom teeth pulled yesterday. " This was a first for praying post-surgery tooth and jaw pain. I asked for Kevin's hand. *"Pain: leave. Gums and jaws: be loose."* I shared a word-thought with Kevin about how God designed him to be a leader and that he has a strong gift of leadership. "That's weird, other people have said that about me."

By this time, LaMont had returned, still as awed as before. I paid for my oil and was again surprised when LaMont and Kevin asked me to meet them in the back where they had parked my car. At times, the hardest risk for me to take is that involving time I had not planned to give. The more I grow with Jesus, the more I realize He seems to rarely be in the same kind of hurry I'm in.

The Holy Spirit began showing me how LaMont once was near to Jesus but had drifted off. Before I even asked LaMont if he wanted to give his life back to Jesus, he began sharing how he once had a thriving walk with Jesus but had drifted off. Instant confirmation. *"Well, do you want to come back to Him right now? His arms are wide open to you!"* His answer was sincere and simple. "Yes, I do. " We held hands and prayed. I gave LaMont my number, email, church info and let him know how Jesus didn't ask people to repeat prayers but to take up their cross and follow Him. Mere moments earlier we were talking about half-naked Miami beaches. *Holy Spirit, You have such a way of working so much with so little.*

Kevin also said he would love to get back to Jesus. Once again I wrote out all my contact info and encouraged him. Come to find out, a local salesman had been watching much of our prayerful conversation and came over to share his story. In the 1970s Johnny had been a biker with Hells Angels. He attested to the night he found Jesus. He had been hit and dragged 200 feet by a fire truck while riding his Harley. The doctors were shocked he survived the crash and gave him zero chance to ever walk again. While in the hospital he had a dream in which Jesus spoke to him and touched his body. The next morning he awoke completely healed. He gave his heart to Jesus right then and there and has been following Him ever since.

I've never had so much fun getting my oil changed—where the longest delay was due to the conversations before, during and after. *Jesus, be praised. Holy Spirit: thank You! Father God, I'm so glad to be Yours.* These risks started with a thought, a word, and ended in the extravagantly generous heart of God toward those He loves by helping me give more freely of my time where I would have otherwise chosen the time-selfishness of a "quick" oil change.

[Risk No. 313, 06/30/2013]
Redbox Rickie.

While trying to make an informed decision for my kids at the Redbox movie stand, Rickie approached me, asking for change to catch a bus. I gave him what I had, a measly $1.50. He seemed grateful enough. I asked his name and how I could pray for him. He had been playing basketball when his cousin landed on his leg, severely breaking a bone in his right leg. He had undergone surgery and months of rehab, but his leg still wasn't right. I prayed for it, commanded pain to leave and bones to be healed. Pain instantly left, and he was stunned. I prayed over his life and thanked God for giving me encouraging words for him.

My friend James walked out of the grocery store and saw Rickie & me praying. Jesus spoke clearly through James to Rickie, and as a result, Rickie handed his life back over to Jesus right then and there. We spent time praying over him and encouraging him. As we returned to the car and told the others the crazy story, we saw Rickie still waiting outside the store. I felt the urge to spend more time with him and invited him to join us for coffee nearby. He agreed and hopped in the passenger seat while everyone else crammed into the back. Awkward introductions and we were off. James covered his bus fare, and we bought Rickie his first ever cold-brewed coffee.

So cool to hang out with Rickie—once a complete stranger—and experience the way each of us was able to express love toward him. It was truly special and a great reminder of how uniquely wired and gifted the body is. Thank You, Jesus.

[Risk No. 760, 08/19/2014]
The Generosity of Name-Asking
& Holy Spirit-Listening.

Lesson number one in the generosity of messy, extravagant risk-taking is treating people as we would like to be treated. Kate was a server where I was meeting a friend for lunch. When I first asked her name, she shared it, and remarked how no one asks—that I had just made her day. Maybe this will be your first risk: "*Hi, I'm Chad. What's your name?*" So many barriers are crossed when we engage in the grace of name asking.

I asked Kate if she was from California. "I am! That's so weird! How did you know that? I haven't lived there for years. Everyone thinks I'm from Georgia. " I shared with her how I saw her with two choices—one being less risky than the other. I saw (in my mind's eye) Jesus pointing her to the riskier option. At this, Kate stopped in her tracks, sat down at the table with me and tried to control herself.

I shared with Kate how as a Jesus-follower, I was learning to hear His voice. I shared how much God loves her, and how part of my job description as a Christian is being sure people experience His love. I sensed tears welling up in my eyes as I shared the love of the Father with her. I then sensed the Holy Spirit sharing with me that she was not yet a believer but He was drawing her and would answer all her doubts and questions about Jesus. She was thrilled and more than happily allowed me to pray with her. I felt pain in my lower back and asked her about it. She immediately said, "My husband. " We took time to pray together for him. What would have been a great lunch with a friend turned into a perfectly timed opportunity to love as I desire to be loved.

[Risk No. 842, 11/17/2014]
Colombia, not Columbia. . .
and Financial Generosity.

On this Sunday, unlike years past, I had not been booked to speak at any area churches. No complaints came from my family on their first trip with me to Colombia. After the crazy, stressful days we had just lived, no complaints came from me either. Our sweet friend, Lina Maria, took us around town on a sunny Colombian Sunday morning.

We landed first at a European-style square (with a *Crepes & Waffles* restaurant—just as delicious as the name suggests) nestled around a quaint neighborhood park. Nidia and Gloria were positioned outside large, ominous doors to the corner Catholic church, marking the centerpiece of the old-world square. Nidia was on crutches and I asked Lina Maria to join me in praying for her. We asked what had happened. Polio had taken over at the age of four. We began praying, both bowed to our knees, not only in reverence to a God who constantly hears, but also for the fact that Nidia was a very small woman and there's something about praying from a position of servant-heartedness over praying *up* while looking *down* on someone.

Church let out nearly the same time we took to praying. I chose to remain in a position of prayer despite the loud mass exiting around me. I could tell many were kindly stopping to give Nidia their change. I opened my eyes once the noise around me subsided. Several bystanders were watching us, others surrounded us in prayer. All pain had left Nidia's body, and she took my hand to take her first crutch-free steps though she was placing significant pressure on my hand.

Nidia then took several steps completely on her own. They were awkward, but they were real. She smiled colossally huge. We purchased bracelets she was selling, encouraged her, hugged, and prayed together for her friend, Gloria. God gave us word-thoughts of encouragement and love for Gloria. Both ladies were in tears as the love of the Father settled on them. So powerful. *Thank You, Jesus.*

I visited my dentist friend in Bogotá the following day to get a chipped tooth looked at. Juan David took quick, quality care of me. I asked if I could offer to pray for any of his other clients while they were waiting in the lobby. I started by offering to pray for his receptionist. She had back pain, and I received a word-thought about a hard time she was having with her father. She was stunned, and God brought healing to both her heart and back.

I prayed for another woman waiting and had a sweet time encouraging her. I noticed Marcela watching me as I prayed over the other ladies. Marcela worked in the insurance business and was waiting to speak with Juan David. I felt God whispering to me about her back having problems. She was healed on the spot and then asked me if I would walk with her to her parked car and pray for her fifteen-year-old son who deals with seizures. *Of course I would. Are you kidding me?* On the way down she informed me her husband wasn't a believer and that he is highly skeptical. Sounds a lot like the former unremarkable me.

Marcela introduced me to her son, Nikolas, and her husband, Mauricio. I said hello and listened as she shared with family how God had just healed her back and that she knew He was there and He was moving. I asked Nikolas if we could pray for him. We all laid hands on him and invited the Holy Spirit to work as He desired. I then felt compelled to share the gospel with Mauricio. I did, and both he and his son expressed their desire to receive Jesus as savior and best friend. At this point, I was beside myself. I've seen God work many wonderful wonders on this risk journey, but people coming spontaneously to Jesus—in the middle of the day—is sweetest of the sweet. At the Holy Spirit's prompting, we all knelt down on rough asphalt parking lot floor, held hands, and invited Jesus to be our everything.

I hugged this beautiful family, encouraged them, and then sensed something strange from the Spirit. I felt Him telling me to give what money I had on me (215,000 Pesos, or about 75 USD) to the couple so they could spend it on a date night. I did, and at these words, both Marcela and her husband began sobbing. She looked at him and said, "I had just been telling God that I so desperately wanted to go on a date with my husband!" God gave me other insights into some financial issues and challenges their marriage was facing.

This family began attending church with my dentist friend and have opened up their home weekly to a small group that meets for prayer and Bible reading. The whole family was transformed by simple steps of obedience. Jesus is amazing.

Maybe you relate well to the phrase, *"Faith is spelled R-I-S-K."*[18] I find faith is also spelled R-E-S-T. Learning to rest is where risk matures most. There are times when I rush into prayer with someone, rather

---

18 John Wimber, https://vineyardusa.org/library/quotes-from-john-wimber/

than pausing, inviting the Holy Spirit to help me, to give me greater compassion, and then just waiting. You will never regret asking the Spirit for help. When you're able to rest in the love God has for you, and everyone else, risks begin looking a whole lot less daunting.

The little prayer I consistently pray, *Jesus, help me to treat even one person today as you would*, prompts me to remember that generosity starts small. Sometimes it even stays small. Don't underestimate the power of God to transform you into the likeness of Jesus.

"From His fullness we have all received, grace upon grace." (John 1:16).

13. When I Get in God's Way.

I have decided to stick with love. Hate is too great a burden to bear.
- *Martin Luther King, Jr.*

God is never limited in His ability to love, but He has limited Himself to make space for you and me. That might sound crazy to you, but His plan was to include, invite and empower regular people to model imperfectly what Jesus demonstrated perfectly. What do I do when I get in the way of God's love for others? When I deliberately choose fear? When bias or judgement is how I see people rather than potential and purpose? Until now, we've covered many aspects of risk-taking, like being empowered by the Holy Spirit, or the conscious awareness that flexibility of your time is often required. What I haven't covered is that each of us carries biases toward one type of person or the next. We all have preconceived assumptions or ideas about certain people that are rarely accurate or representative of how God sees them. On my journey in the messy, extravagant new, I've found one of my weaknesses is in how I relate to, or understand, the LGBT community.

Jesus loves lesbians. And gays, bisexuals, transgender individuals, those wondering identity—sexual or asexual—and all those whose identity is wandering. I sometimes struggle to love like Jesus. Every last one of us, at one point or another, and in one way or another, has wrestled with identity. Jesus loved us in confusion and loves us in stability. His life on Earth was repeatedly shared with the ones who were judged, marginalized, and shunned by the religious elite. The Bible teaches us that God hates divorce (Malachi 2:16), yet when a woman caught sleeping with someone else's husband was brought to Jesus, He didn't condemn, much less hate. He demonstrated love.

The scribes and the Pharisees brought a woman who had been caught in adultery, and placing her in the midst they said to him, "Teacher, this woman has been caught in the act of adultery. Now in the Law Moses commanded us to stone such women. So what do you say?" This they said to test him, that they might have some charge to bring against him. Jesus bent down and wrote with his finger on the ground. And as they continued to ask him, he stood up and said to them, "Let him who is without sin among you be the first to throw a stone at her." And once more he bent down and wrote on the ground. But when they heard it, they went away one by one, beginning with the older ones, and Jesus was left alone with the woman standing before him. Jesus stood up and said to her, "Woman, where are they? Has no one condemned you?" She said, "No one, Lord." And Jesus said, "Neither do I condemn you; go, and from now on sin no more." (John 8:3-11).

Where was the man? It's the single most obvious question I've never heard asked on this passage. Was he not caught with the woman? Last I heard, adultery required consenting pairs. Just like the first man God created—Adam—it's always easier to blame Eve than take ownership for our own shortcomings. The second thing spinning in my brain is what Jesus may have written in the dirt. Speculation runs everywhere from the sins of those spiritual leaders present to something so silly as buying Himself time to collect His thoughts. The Bible doesn't tell us what He wrote so the best answer is in His response. Regardless of what was written, it only required one compassion-crammed challenge to send accusers scurrying. *"Let him who is without sin among you be the first to throw a stone at her."* The story ends with Jesus saying, *"and from now on sin no more."* Jesus forgives sinners and then empowers us to leave our wrongs behind.

Beth and I were recently invited to a wedding reception for friends who are lesbians. Our friends were planning a wedding in California with a reception back home in Nashville. Time passed awkwardly by as I swung back and forth on what to do, from sensing I should go to determining I couldn't. Or wouldn't. At one point, Beth and I were outright asked if we could make it to the reception. Beth, in her typical quick-witted style, said we weren't sure as there was so much going on in our lives that same weekend (which was true). I, on the other hand, made up a quick white lie of a story about having my brother and his family in town. True—only to a degree. My brother and his family had invited us to spend time with them, but I knew it was days out from the actual Saturday night reception. I was wrong. White lie sins are no less insulting to God or others than any other mistake I'm likely to commit.

The reception was exactly one week out. I was enjoying the South's hot, humid summer mornings while stretching my legs on a neighborhood run. Until this run, I had continued swinging from attending to avoiding, the latter being the position I was holding fast to. Then, while on my run, Jesus' still-small-voice spoke to me: "Why wouldn't you go?" His question forced me to analyze my reasons for *and* against. The reasons against simply boiled down to one major concern: fear that I couldn't celebrate a homosexual choice because I didn't believe a homosexual lifestyle was endorsed by God.

God's best for us in marriage—and in life—is when we submit and surrender to His good, pleasing, perfect will in Christ Jesus. Jesus is the example; He is the model. Without Him, *One Thousand Risks* is just a random book on some bizarre social experiment. Is it possible for Christians to be gay? Of course it is. Is it possible for Christians to be many things and yet not please God in or through them? Absolutely.

The problem is when our identity, no matter the area (LGBTQIA+

lifestyles just happen to be today's hot topic and a relevant group to share my own challenges from), influences our hearts louder than God's Word and Spirit. As a Christian, you may also be a habitual liar, though you're called to be truthful. This doesn't make you a lying Christian but a Christian who lies. The difference is drastic. If you have given your life to Jesus, invited Him to live within you, you are a blood-purchased Christian before anything else. You may be a saint who sometimes sins, but you are not a sinner who sometimes saints.

Why wouldn't I go to the wedding reception? I feared our presence would serve as an endorsement for a decision I didn't feel I could support as someone who holds a traditional view that the Bible means what it says. How could I, in clear conscience, congratulate a couple for something I didn't feel God was congratulating? My mind had already rehearsed the night many times over. "Ladies and gentlemen, I present to you Mrs. and Mrs." At that trumpeting announcement, all would stand, clap, and cheer. But could I clap, even a half-hearted clap, for a decision I did not believe was biblically right?

I even believed a lesbian/homosexual relationship was wrong. Sin. Yes, I did just mean to use the "s" word. How could I try to be real with you in every way, except for when it comes to cultural-majority challenges like this? I did not use the word "sin" out of spiteful bitterness or evil anger, but purely from a heart postured by theological conviction. I might be foolish, but I'm not an idiot. I know what I'm writing here is highly unpopular. Still, I would rather write you one hard thing I was convinced you needed to hear over 99 easy things that would do you no good.

My point in this chapter is not to shout my opinion on homosexuality or to give you all six Bible verses that clearly *do not* condone homosexual actions, but to be transparent with you on an area I struggle with. If you google the phrase, "what did Jesus say about homosexuality" you will get approximately 641,000 responses while the similar phrase, "what did Jesus say about love" will land you over 52 million results. At least according to Google, understanding what Jesus says about love is 81 times more interesting than what He didn't say about homosexuality (which is true, Jesus did not actually talk about homosexuality that we know of). My point is that Jesus loves and commanded me to love. He does not cuddle, condone or celebrate my messy issues (of which there are plenty), but he invites me into liberating extravagance.

The longer I live *in* love the easier it is to *recognize* fear. I sensed fear in my answer to Jesus' pointed question on why I wouldn't attend the lesbian wedding reception. I confessed and apologized. In that moment, I had my answer. Peace and confidence had caught up to me. Later that same day, I shared my Jesus conversation with Beth. She seemed somewhat surprised but was kind enough to trust my spiritual intuition.

The following is my note that was placed along with a gift to our friends:

Sarah & Tina,

We are grateful for you. Beth and I consider your lives a gift—from God to the world broadly and to each of us personally. Thank you for inviting us a bit closer to your hearts and story.

As Christians living in the buckle of the "Bible belt" I realize stereotypes and assumptions are often stronger forces than love itself. When we received your invitation, I wrestled with what to do. As cliché as it may sound, I asked Jesus, in prayer, what He would do.

The response I felt He brought to my heart was this: Of course I would go! Sarah and Tina have already heard the megaphones loudly opposing their relationship, often in My name. I didn't instruct My followers to point out all those areas of potential disagreement, or to wave the banners of who's right and who's wrong. I demonstrated—by My life and death—that those who follow Me were called to live radical examples of love. Perfect love displaces fear.

I pray Beth & I will serve your lives by a love more committed and concerned for you than any fear-agenda against you.

It's a privilege to know you.

Chad & Beth

We attended the reception, unsure of what to expect or how the evening would go, yet fully convinced Jesus would go regardless of who might misunderstand our motives. I hugged. I prayed. I interceded in tongues under my breath for those around me. I guarded my words to guard my conscience. I didn't say, "Congratulations," I said, "It's wonderful to see you, we love you, and we're grateful for you." The emphasis is always— and especially when we don't agree—*love.*

The following story was an experience I had with several *YWAM* leader-friends who invited me to dinner while I was teaching at their base outside Denver. Aaron, our waiter, stood out to me as nervous, odd, starving artist, and probably gay. It sounds horrible admitting how quickly I was able to stereotype, even judge, someone I'd barely met. Jesus, forgive me.

At one point during a spicy, remarkably fantastic Buffalo-sausage, green-chili ravioli dish, one of the *YWAM* leaders asked which spiritual gift I wrestle with most. *Genius* question. All of them? The gift of prophecy is probably where I struggle most, but I want to keep growing in all nine. "For example," I said, "I've been asking Jesus for His thoughts toward our waiter, and I'm coming up blank. I've got nothing."Moments before we paid our bill I had the faint, but clear mind-picture, of the words "audio" and "technica" along with a turntable spinning vintage vinyl. I shared the thought with my table and told them this would be a great example of what messy, awkward risk-taking looks like. The only thing I considered was that maybe Aaron was thinking about opening a record store or doing some kind of technical audio work.

When Aaron again came by to check on us I explained how we were all Christians learning to hear God's voice for others. I asked if he would give me his permission to share my thoughts. He agreed. I shared the words and the picture of the record player spinning vintage records. As soon as I began suggesting how the picture/words might connect to him, Aaron abruptly interrupted me by saying, "I can stop you right there." This was when I winked at the group around me knowing full well what I was about to hear. Never could I have anticipated what Aaron spoke next: "My mother was the most important person in my life. She just died. The last thing I did with her before she passed was play old records on a turntable. Oh, my goodness. I don't even know what to say or do right now."

Aaron—showing obviously anxious, edgy energy—turned around suddenly and walked out of the room. In the same instant, compassion moved us to a deep, collective awe. We were all wiping tears from our cheeks. I went from judging someone to thinking I was crazy to being as shocked as anyone that Jesus had just spoken to Aaron where he was hurting most. On Aaron's return, he told us he wasn't a Christian but that he was genuinely shocked and had begun attending church where his boyfriend sings in the choir. Aaron kindly agreed as we asked permission to pray over him. We held hands, praying over a heart obviously distraught from the loss of his mother, inviting Jesus to continue restoring. We hugged and thanked Aaron for being so open with us. Only Jesus perfectly meets someone like Aaron at the intersection where need and healing converge. I walked out repenting and apologizing for the way I had perceived our server and thanked God for moving through even a wayward fool like me.

On my return flight home from the same trip that birthed the preceding story, my neighbor and I were both upgraded to seats 10A and 10B. As soon as I sat down it dawned on me that this upgrade may have been more curse than blessing. Janet shared how thrilled she was to meet up with her wife in Nashville for a weekend of music and drinking. Proving how slowly I learn, I once again found myself stereotyping and tending far more toward judgement than mercy. I had met my match in talkers with the gift of gab as Janet showed no signs of slowing down.

I asked God for more grace and an opportunity to share Him with her. He's so kind. Somehow we began talking ISIS and radical Islam (specifically how brutal they stand against lesbians and gays). I told Janet that I had been to the Middle East on a few occasions but never anywhere extremely close to ISIS. She found it interesting that both they and I could call our actions the "will of God." I went on to explain that if I were to visit ISIS they would count severing my head from my body an act of obedience the same as I would consider laying my life down for the gospel.

This was the door that led our conversation toward why Jesus is different than every other religion, even the "religion" of Christianity. I explained relationship and intimacy. Both Janet's brothers are pastors though she had taken a very different path. She seemed to grasp how Jesus was claiming something very different than the religious ideal of works. I asked Janet if I could share several "prophetic" word-thoughts I felt God was placing on my heart. She responded with a confident "sure." She leaned in closer to me and listened intently. I was stunned by how our conversation had started and where it currently had morphed. Once I shared my "Jesus-thoughts" (which she responded whole-heartedly excited to) I asked about pain in her right shoulder. She confirmed but then motioned to her left shoulder and shared the story of two days prior having fallen on her left side with pain at a nine out of ten on the scale. I told Janet about the gift of words of knowledge and how sometimes the

Holy Spirit will speak to me through pain I'm feeling in my own body for a healing He desires to bring about in someone else. I instructed Janet to place her right hand on her left shoulder while I laid my hand on her right shoulder. I welcomed peace and commanded pain to leave then asked her to test her shoulder. She began moving and then looked my way with an absurd, confounded smile. "It feels like my whole left side is hot and there's no pain at all anymore." I laughed. Of course. Twice now, people I had marginalized, stereotyped, even judged on the basis of outward actions, appearances or commentary were the ones Jesus seemed exceedingly willing to touch. We hugged. Janet thanked me for a moment as profound as ours and told me how thrilled she was to share the story with her wife.

Though I may not agree with Sarah, Tina, Aaron or Janet's actions/decisions/lifestyles, in each case I walked away apologizing to Jesus for not having looked at them *first* through the filter of love. Not for a second in any of these encounters did Jesus give me the impression that people were a problem He was afraid of. All this to say, growing is necessary and required. I have a long road ahead of me, but as long as growth happens, I'm ecstatic at the prospect of loving more and not less.

14. Revival.

Light yourself on fire with passion and people will come from miles to watch you burn.

- John Wesley

Two pursuits have encouraged me most when it comes to growing a life of passion.

First, reading what the Bible says *about* the Holy Spirit—like pouring over the Book of Acts and noting every time the Holy Spirit was mentioned or referenced—praying I would have eyes to see and ears to hear. I remember being struck by the first time the Holy Spirit was mentioned; *"after He (Jesus) through the Holy Spirit had given commandments. . .".* What commandments did Jesus give *through* the Holy Spirit to his apostles? He told them not to leave Jerusalem; to wait on the Promise. Jesus *promised* the Holy Spirit of the Father. The second thing Jesus said about the Spirit in the Book of Acts was that John had baptized with water, but the Holy Spirit would baptize them in power. Jesus even told his disciples earlier (John 16:7) that it was actually to their advantage He departed, otherwise the Helper would not come.

In an exchange far greater than my brain's capacity to process, Jesus' life, death, resurrection, and return to Heaven served as the complete set of keys unlocking the Holy Spirit to us. Huge beyond comprehension. The Holy Spirit is not some mysterious "it" or a weird cosmic force. He is the personality of God aimed exclusively at convicting sinners and empowering saints toward bringing honor to Jesus.

Second, discovering what the Holy Spirit accomplished in times and ages *past*, along with what He is actively up to *now*—specifically in connection to revival and those He flows through to deliver God's Kingdom on earth. Revival, by my estimation, is any time the manifest presence of God so heavily materializes on earth that no human logic can explain the resulting reactions.

Revival rarely seems to happen the same way twice, but it always appears marked by a deep *groaning* for more of God coupled with the reality of our brokenness. In other words, we need Him more than we need anything else. Biblical revival, great awakenings of the Holy Spirit, where entire nations—like China[19]—come to Jesus with such thundering repentance all of Heaven hears and rejoices. I dream of revival.

Rarely has God given me visions, but He did—on July 26th, 2008— the same summer He used three different individuals, at three unique, unrelated times to prophesy my departure from conventional music into messy extravagance. I was in Albuquerque, NM. The time was 11PM, just after my friends had finished their worship sets.

I received a mind-picture of a huge body of water. Very still, placid water. A massive man-made dam was holding the water back. The dam appeared to have been in place for years and years. It was enormous, stretching for miles. On the dry side of the dam I noticed cracks and fissures, indicating the dam's aging weakness.

Again, I saw the body of water held back by the dam, though this time I noticed one of the cracks leaking a small, steady stream of water. The third, final "picture" I received came accompanied by a still-small inner voice saying, "Look, and see what I will be doing. " My eyes were drawn to the body of water being held back by a weakening dam, and then, in

---

19 http://www.christianitytoday.com/edstetzer/2017/june/china-house-churches-and-growth-of-kingdom.html

a mere instant, the pressure caused by the weight of the water crushed the dam, overwhelming it into millions of broken pieces. Huge swells of water rushed out over a green, hilly land where nothing in its path was left untouched. Trees were uprooted. Boulders were carried away. The massive flow of water poured forth with such ferocity that nothing could stop it.

At the time, I didn't fully understand what the body of water symbolized but sensed God explaining it to me later, in a time of prayer, as His body of believers, specifically youth. These young lives, with 1 Corinthians 1:27 in mind, would uproot years of man-made opposition to His plan: *"But God chose what is foolish in the world to shame the wise; God chose what is weak in the world to shame the strong. . . "*

I believe a movement is coming where youth especially, though not exclusively, will live in complete abandon to everything but the power of the Holy Spirit guiding them toward Jesus. It's already happening, though maybe not yet in terms defined by the quantity of my dreaming. God is reaching youth at a profound core where previous generations had not considered yielding or going. Whether you are young or old, I pray you and I would live as though the end were upon us. May God fill your heart with a hunger for the kingdom of God and His righteousness.

On Good Friday of Easter weekend 2009, less than a year after God gave me the vision of the dam, He provided me with a wild confirmation unlike anything I've experienced before or since.

While driving from Orange County, CA to Los Angeles with my good friend, Graham, our navigation system suddenly and unexpectedly rerouted us from Interstate 5 to Interstate 405, though we could see signs for Los Angeles directly in front of us. We quickly discussed and decided to follow our GPS system which we lovingly referred to as "Janet." Janet led us through a maze of industrial parks for several minutes before landing us at an on-ramp to the 405. Standing on the side of the on-ramp were two young men who looked rough-around-the-edges with their thumbs sticking out. Graham immediately blurted out Jim Carrey's line from the movie *Dumb and Dumber*, "Pick 'em up!"

Because I hadn't seen the movie I didn't realize Graham was only joking so that by the time he explained the movie reference we had already pulled off to the side of the highway on-ramp and the young men were moving toward us. They clambered into the backseat of our rental car right as Graham and I looked at each other with the same mischievous kingdom-thought, *we're going to share Jesus with these hobo hitch-hiking young guns. They have no idea what they're in for.*

We asked where they were headed and freaked out when they responded with, "Northern California, though we had hoped to make a Good Friday service at Calvary Chapel Costa Mesa." We were floored and beyond shocked to learn they, too, were followers of Jesus. As we continued talking they informed us that they were from Albuquerque, New Mexico and that God had sent them on a crazy mission to leave everything behind, trusting only Him for provision as needs arose. I was bewildered when they said, "We've been better fed and provided for on this hitch-hiking journey than ever in our lives."

On discovering they were from Albuquerque, I shared how I loved their city and had visited on several occasions while touring with my artist friends in *The Glorious Unseen* and *Sleeping Giant*. At this they let out a shout and a huge "no way!"

Excitedly, they began drilling me on which show I had been to and whether it was in such and such a building. As it turns out, Graham and I had just picked up two hitchhikers who had been at the exact same show that I had been at only a few months prior.

Then they recounted the story that ultimately led them to our car. Jesus had begun challenging them to greater obedience when they both decided to attend the same *Sleeping Giant* show that I had "ironically" also been present for.

"Yeah man! So we were at this show, and during the middle of one of the bands, some random guy was given the microphone out in the middle of the crowd and he dropped to his knees, crying his heart out to God. As soon as we heard him praying we knew Jesus was calling us to forsake everything and follow after Him. This whole journey we're on is a direct result of whoever that was praying!"

At this point, I almost drove off the highway into a ditch for feeling the presence of God in a way that I still feel now while writing this eight years later. I looked at Graham and then back at the young men in my rearview mirror and asked if they wanted to hear something crazy.

"I was THAT random guy on his knees crying out to God!!!!"

As you can imagine, our car erupted, and we marveled at what kind of impossible odds God must have worked together toward pulling off a moment as unique and set apart like this. We invited our new friends to stay the night with us in Los Angeles and to travel up the coast to San Luis Obispo for what became one of the most outrageous, memorable weekends of my life.

Advance the kingdom of God, awaken the world to the love of Jesus.

Many times, we Christians pray things like, "Jesus, please come back today because I'm miserable and don't want to face another one of life's minutes." Though Heaven sounds more appealing some days than others, that's about as selfish a prayer as has ever been uttered. What we ought to be praying is, "Jesus, please delay for the sake of global revival, of those who have yet to hear." Misery for the believer is a short-term, temporary discomfort. Misery for the non-believer is a permanent, eternal separation from God. How could I not be petitioning God for Jesus' delay until everyone has had a clear opportunity to hear and see the gospel of the kingdom?

God, break our hearts for the lost. Break my heart. Break me down.

Give me a compassion for the hurting—and a passion for revival—that could only come from You. Forgive me for being so selfish and uncaring. Father, I pray for my reader in this very moment. Help them know that, of all the treasures in life, You are to be cherished most. Encourage hearts; renew minds. Give eyes to see and ears to hear what the Spirit is saying today. Forgive them—forgive me—for how quickly we abandon the ways of the Spirit. Holy Spirit, touch this writer. Touch this reader. I surrender fresh. Here we are, send us. Here are my dreams, life-longings, hopes. I lay them at Your feet. Make of them what You know is best. Help us to grow together in joy-fueled obedience. Pour out Your Holy Spirit on us in such a way that we couldn't help but bring messy, extravagant fire.

15. The Greatest Risk, The Greatest Wonder.

So whether for light or for ashes, all of us burn for something.

- Jonah Matranga

Consequently, he is able to save to the uttermost those who draw near to God through him, since he always lives to make intercession for them. Who is to condemn? Christ Jesus is the one who died—more than that, who was raised—who is at the right hand of God, who indeed is interceding for us. My little children, I am writing these things to you so that you may not sin. But if anyone does sin, we have an advocate with the Father, Jesus Christ the righteous. For there is one God, and there is one mediator between God and men, the man Christ Jesus... Since then we have a great high priest who has passed through the heavens, Jesus, the Son of God, let us hold fast our confession. For we do not have a high priest who is unable to sympathize with our weaknesses, but one who in every respect has been tempted as we are, yet without sin. Let us then with confidence draw near to the throne of grace, that we may receive mercy and find grace to help in time of need. For through him we both have access in one Spirit to the Father. - Bible verses taken from April 6th's morning reading of Daily Light on the Daily Path.

I held myself together for nearly two hours, a feat I was more than impressed with. In one unexpected, climactic moment—what some would call weakness—all that holding together, turned to river-running sobs. I wept uncontrollably. I bowed my head and shook with a cry that possessed my soul deeper than I could possibly comprehend. There I sat, overwhelmed with not an ounce of willpower capable enough to deliver me. Cameras rolled unfazed as a still veiled, yet former, Muslim girl sat calmly controlled across the table from me.

Stories are meant to be as interesting as those who live them. In this case, Stefanie's (for her and her family's safety I am not using her real name) story was the most miraculous account of healing and salvation I've personally come across. Her countenance spoke from a realm beyond compelling—externally, the surroundings fit her well—but internally she was the farthest thing from common. My shoulders were covered by gentle, assuring hands and tissues piled over in an effort to soak my tears. When I finally regained mild composure, our eyes met, and she released a genuine sensitivity in the form of "I'm sorry."

Stefanie, a bright twenty-one-year-old Lebanese university student, likely filled barrels with tears she once shed. Now she was growing accustomed to the way listeners were responding. The only words going through my heart in that space were, "Holy. Holy. Holy. The Lord God almighty is holy. I must decrease so He can increase."

It was on a hot, humid evening, July 2015, in Beirut, Lebanon when I discovered just how unlikely it was Stephanie and I even met. First, Stephanie had originally planned to travel abroad with a good friend, starting exactly at the time we arrived. Plans fell through, and she opted to stay home. Second, since her miracle on May 19th, 2014, she had received three interview requests from major networks offering to tell her story. She turned them all down for the simple fact that she did not feel peace.

When our Swiss friend working in Lebanon, Lukas, texted to ask if a random bunch of guys could interview her, she did what first came to mind and what she had done three times prior. She emailed her psychologist (whom she had met during her illness and grown in friendship with since) to seek counsel. Her psychologist responded by encouraging her to do what she felt best. Much to my excitement, she agreed to an interview. What Stefanie gave my heart could only have come from the hope of glory Himself.

Stefanie had avoided a lump in her right breast for months. When she finally had it checked, her doctor acted quickly to have what turned out to be a cancerous mass removed. Chemotherapy ensued. Months into the chemo process, a second lump was discovered and removed. Though she had grown up as the eldest daughter in a strong Muslim household surrounded by five younger brothers, Stefanie had routinely questioned God's existence. All this sickness had further flushed Him away.

Cancer moved from bad to horrible when she began noticing a heaviness in the back of her head along with symptoms she had not experienced with breast cancer or chemo. Stefanie returned to her doctor where her father, in complete disbelief, requested three separate tests (in addition to a second opinion) to confirm a cancerous tumor indeed was growing in her central nervous system (CNS). Before this devastating discovery, she was largely on the mend. Friends and family had begun congratulating her for having beaten beastly cancer.

Now Stefanie's fragile world crumbled at the shock her doctor was revealing. He was giving her an estimated seven months to live. Not only had she experienced breast cancer, but now she was victim to one of the rarest forms of cancer known to man, near guaranteed by medical science to end her life prematurely.

In utter disbelief, Stefanie began making plans to squeeze in several final life goals—scuba diving, skydiving, bungee jumping, spending Christmas in Italy, enjoying family and friends as much as possible. During this season, she began experiencing intensified symptoms bringing near constant and extreme pain, memory loss, temporary blindness, paralysis, and sleeplessness—in which, at one point, she suffered nine days without sleeping a single second. Sleep was the one time she could avoid pain even strong meds weren't curbing. Suicide became an option she seriously contemplated to end her suffering.

Stefanie was as broken as they come when her doctor offered a sliver of hope—an ultra-high-risk, extremely low-outcome surgery that had only been performed several times in all of history—the last time being in 2001. The surgery offered a 0. 028 percent success rate. Surgery presented a tiny glimmer worth agreeing to hope for. Odds were 99. 97% she would die on the surgical table. The surgery would be performed on May 20th, 2014 at a hospital in Los Angeles (where her doctor in Beirut had formerly worked). The hospital required a family member to arrive early to set paperwork and logistics in order. The medical community waited with anticipation as Stefanie had granted permission for a surgery that could help change the future of medicine in this area. Doctors would be able to learn from her procedure whether she lived or died.

This is where the paragraphs turn supernaturally bizarre. A month prior to the scheduled surgery, a good friend had unexpectedly entered the unlikely doors of a tiny Christian bookstore in downtown Beirut. Stefanie's friend had hopes of finding a special gift for her in this time of heavy distress. While perusing the shelves, she began crying. Several people who volunteered at the bookstore asked what was wrong and why she was crying. She went on to explain her good friend's fight. They prayed for Stefanie though she wasn't present and shared how they'd love to pray again if she were to bring Stefanie by at some point.

By May 19th, Stefanie's father was already in Los Angeles preparing for what I can only imagine being the hardest thing any father could ever do—holding a shred of hopeful optimism knowing well the odds that within a day his first child, and only daughter, would die. My daughter is my eldest child. She's incredible. I can't even comprehend the idea, let alone being in the situation itself.

Back home in Beirut, Stefanie's good friend had told her she had a surprise for her and wanted to spend a little time with her before she left for LA. Stefanie only desired to spend what little time she had left at home with close friends and family members. Her friend insisted. Without having a clue to the back story, they walked into the same humble Christian bookstore. Stefanie immediately asked her friend why in the world they were in a store that was obviously selling Jesus material. That's when Hiam (owner of the bookstore and spiritual mom to countless many in Lebanon and beyond) asked what she could do for the two. "This is my friend, Stefanie, who I told you about. She's leaving for California tomorrow morning. I brought her here for prayer."

Hiam and those with her began explaining the power of Jesus, His death, and His resurrection. Knowing that they would likely never see Stefanie again, Hiam boldly asked if she would like to invite Jesus to enter her heart and take ownership of her life. "Sure. Why not?" came Stefanie's quick, willing response.

Hiam assumed Stefanie must have misunderstood her. "No, Jesus died for you. He loves you. He rose from death for you. He is alive, and He is more than a prophet, He is the Son of—and only way to—God. Do you want to receive Him?" "Yes, of course. I have nothing to lose." Stefanie knew better than anyone a last-ditch effort was better than no effort at all.

Right there, Stefanie took an extravagant risk. She invited Jesus, King of the Universe, to enter her life and make all things new. She didn't recall feeling anything extraordinary in the moment other than peace. Later that night, surrounded by a house full of mourning, hurting family, she felt the need to be alone. She knew it was weird to be alone, especially considering her limited time, but kindly asked her mother, brothers, aunts, cousins and others to leave her room. At first they fought her desire to be secluded, but Stefanie was able to convince them she just wanted a little time to think. When they all exited the room, she laid down on her bed and began feeling a weight being lifted from her body.

Before she knew it, her family was surrounding her with surprised eyes wide. She hadn't slept for days, not even for a minute. Somehow she had managed to fall asleep for two hours before her family rushed in concerned at what may have happened. Unbelievably, Stefanie slept the remainder of the night, waking the next morning to an obvious realization that the pressure and weight in the back of her head was gone.

In the morning, Stefanie drove to the hospital where the plan had been to meet her doctor then leave together for the airport. Since he was to perform the surgery, he had kindly offered to personally accompany her to Los Angeles. Once with her doctor, he opted to run a final set of tests to compare with previous ones. Again, her case was so rare that anything they could learn was an added bonus. He ran a test then sat down with her, results in hand. He explained how there must have been something wrong with the test, or the machine that ran the test, as the levels, once erratically all over the place, were reading zero in every category.

He quickly ordered a CT scan of her brain to measure the tumor and then called Stefanie over to compare the two scans. He showed her previous scans (you'll recall her father had three separate exams ordered because he didn't want to believe his precious daughter had a brain tumor). Stefanie's doctor was speechless. The tumor that had once been so clearly detected was now not even present in the slightest form. Her doctor ordered yet another exam, which confirmed that every level in her body was normal. They both stood shocked.

Instead of flying to Los Angeles to meet her heartbroken father, she called him on the phone to share the unbelievable news that her doctor had pronounced her 100% cured. Her father literally fainted. He (later) ordered a second round of three separate tests because he couldn't believe it was true—each one came back clear. What was meant to be a near-certain funeral procession transformed into a joyous roar of life-celebration.

No one could believe what had happened. It had all been so simple. Stefanie invited Jesus to be her Lord and Savior. Hiam and her team had prayed for her healing, but she hadn't expected anything to change. Now they had to deal with the awkward situations of her father flying back to Beirut, Stefanie and her doctor not showing for their flight, or a surgery that an entire team of specialists were preparing for. When I asked Stefanie if she and her doctor were reimbursed for their airfare, she proudly chimed, "No. But what's an airfare compared to this miracle?"

I interviewed Stefanie and spent hours more sharing my heart and hearing hers. We talked non-profits, Jesus, what it's like to be healed by Jesus, and the response of a family where not a single member proclaimed Christ prior to Stefanie's miracle. As of my interview with her (July 20th, 2015) one of her prayer goals was her entire family coming to Jesus.

In addition to Stefanie's story, I met countless others while in Lebanon who have had equally powerful Jesus encounters. In this culture, where religion (in the forms of Islam, Christianity and the eighteen or more sects between them) is fought over, argued over, even killed over, I wasn't hearing people talk about how they were coming to Jesus because theological understanding had finally set in. Middle Eastern youth were claiming to have *experienced* Jesus. In dreams. Visions. Supernatural encounters. "As a Father that held my hand and walked with me as though I was his son." In hearing His *still, small* voice or hearing His outright *audible* voice. Sometimes repenting on the spot with fear and trembling—having never even heard the Gospel message other than Jesus appearing to them—in person.

Stephanie's friend took risks in visiting a Christian bookstore, admitting why she was distraught, inviting prayer, and ultimately bringing

Stephanie to the store. Hiam, and the other bookstore employees, took risks by sharing the Gospel with Stephanie and praying healing over her body. Stephanie's greatest risk and greatest wonder was entrusting her heart to Jesus.

If we refuse to grow in the awkward, awesome of risk-taking, fear will become a close friend, and we won't live empowered by the Spirit. Where the gospel isn't preached, rarely do people come to Jesus. Where the sick aren't prayed for, rarely is anyone healed. Had the earliest followers of Jesus, the disciples themselves, not been willing to develop lives of risk—had they rather stayed and prayed in safe rooms—how would the billions of Christians over the past 2,000+ years, like you and me, have met Jesus?

Not living by the Spirit means we miss the greatest adventure on the planet. What if every one of us Christians took only one risk to love God and neighbors as we love ourselves? How much would our own experience, not to mention the whole global world, turn upside down? Jesus is the one we're after. Live bright, passionately focused, like nothing matters nearly as much as bringing glory to God. Love whomever God places in front of you and watch how He moves impossibilities aside. Be a light shining in the darkness and witness darkness being swallowed up by light. Psalm 40:5 says, *You have multiplied, O Lord my God, your wondrous deeds and your thoughts toward us; none can compare with you! I will proclaim and tell of them yet they are more than can be told.* Share your stories, write them down, document your journey. Inspire the world by your radical commitment to follow Jesus wherever He leads you. Be willing to step through fear, into what the world calls foolish for what Jesus deems treasure.

If God can move through me, He can *flow* through you. One thing Jesus never promised was easy. Don't quit. And if you have given up on Jesus, be honest about where you're not, repent and return to the Father's arms that are waiting wide open to receive you. Keep going. You're armed with kingdom potential; after all, your Father is King of the Universe.

You've just finished reading story after story of God moving me out of the way to love my neighbors more. Now it's your turn. You are never alone, the Spirit of Truth is always present, even when you may be feeling otherwise. You belong, you matter, you've been adopted out of fear into the glorious, hopeful riches of Christ.

He doesn't need you to be the most gifted evangelist to powerfully speak the Gospel. You don't have to be the most anointed member of the body to bring healing to someone's hurts. Offer to pray for people anywhere you go, listen to the Spirit, and watch God astound you by His power.

The seventy-two returned with joy, saying, "Lord, even the demons are subject to us in your name!" And he said to them, "I saw Satan fall like lightning from heaven. Behold, I have given you authority to tread on serpents and scorpions, and over all the power of the enemy, and nothing shall hurt you." (Luke 10:17-19). Jesus invited us to leave the *unremarkable old* for a messy, extravagant new. Even more than witnessing His power flowing through your weakness, know that your name is written in the Lamb's book of life. Forever glory.

"Nevertheless, do not rejoice in this, that the spirits are subject to you, but rejoice that your names are written in heaven." (Luke 10:20).

To join this *One Thousand Risks* all-out revolt on fear, simply take one.

Fear is not your friend.

P.S.:

Thank you for having finished my book. What an absolute honor to have you here! Hopefully, it's evident by now, but I enjoy writing. I'd love for my life to continue serving yours, so I've included five "next-steps" for you to consider.

1. Download the bonus *One Thousand Risks* Resource-Pack, including three instant digital guides aimed at helping you imagine and experience the messy, extravagant new:

- *The Risk-Taker's Roadmap: 14 Steps To Developing A Life of Risk.*
- *Q&A: My 15 Most Frequently Asked Questions on Risk-Taking.*
- *Destination: B-Stories* (Because I can only include so many words here).

2. Read all (or even a couple) of the original *One Thousand Risks* blog posts at *onethousandrisks.com.*

3. Please visit *chadisliving.com* to download the bonuses above and so we can fight fear together.

4. Join my weekly e-mail list and receive exclusive opportunities to travel the world with me, encouraging tales, along with thoughts on how to develop a more profound love for Jesus and neighbor.

5. *Come&Live!* is a worldwide community committed to the idea of using art and music to change the world for Jesus. The *C&L!* community is not only for artists and creatives, but anyone and everyone with a passion for seeing Christian artists inspired to reach Global Youth Culture for Jesus. If you're an artist or creative, who is using your gifts to share the gospel outside the church, *Come&Live!* would love to get to know you! You can join our community and/or apply to become a *Come&Live!* artist at *comeandlive.com.*

Footnotes.

1. Acts 15:25&26, Romans 16:3&4, Philippians 2:29&30, respectively
2. https://www.youtube.com/watch?v=YUW3hsBH790
3. The Book of Acts Chapter 8, verses 26-40
4. https://en.wikipedia.org/wiki/Christianity
5. http://creationwiki.org/Phobia#cite_note-2
6. www.onethousandrisks.com
7. The Book of John 15:18
8. James 1:22
9. *Rolling Stone* news article, dated 05/16/2014.
10. https://youtu.be/y7HfCN0YqAU
11. http://www.grace-abounding.com/Articles/Sin/Pride_Edwards. htm
12. The Book of Luke 4:40
13. The Book of Matthew 5:43-45
14. 1 Peter 1:16, reference
15. https://www.nytimes.com/2016/06/29/travel/is-istanbul-safe-what-travelers-should-know. html
16. https://en.wikipedia. org/wiki/Islam_in_Turkey
17. https://en.wikipedia. org/wiki/Protestantism_in_Turkey
18. John Wimber, https://vineyardusa.org/library/quotes-from-john-wimber/
19. http://www.christianitytoday.com/edstetzer/2017/june/china-house-churches-and-growth-of-kingdom.html

Acknowledgements.

My love, honor, and appreciation to everyone listed below go farther than any word-scribbling could ever express.

To Beth, Sydney & David: thank you for not only living life with me, but loving me in all of my colorful, bizarre, quirky expressions. My Keeyaaa's! Kotseee, kotsee!

To my team of editors: Darcie Clemen (developmental editing), Ken Darrow (copy editing), and Kendall Davis (proofreading): You've helped shape ideas and words into a book carrying more weight than I could have possibly hoped for. My sincerest gratitude!

To my Beth: Your hand aggressively striking, in red pencil, paragraph after paragraph was the most beautiful gift you could have ever given my writing process. I finally finished. Thank you.

My parents and siblings: You have consistently modeled unconditional love to me over the years. Thank you for believing in your eldest son/brother. You all inspire me.

Team Johnson: You have been the financial and spiritual team enabling me to live this crazy expression of faith, without you I would never have known the definition of generosity. My heart goes out to you at the deepest level for the way in which each of you are sacrificially and joyfully giving to my family and me. I am forever grateful to be with you in the race. (Note: if you're interested in talking with me about joining this team, please email me - chad@comeandlive.com).

Immanuel Nashville: Thank you, Ray & TJ, for welcoming someone as unique as me and for helping inspire this book at the core level. Thank you to all the elders and deacons, the global missions team, and everyone else who has been such a gift to our family.

Jason Cheek: #Doyouevennativetonguebro.

Stacey Allen: I am so thankful for your perseverance and willingness to read my entire first draft and yet still provide me with massively undeserved encouragement.

James Allen: May all our future "business" meetings be conducted while waiting at or near a Koi pond. You've been a remarkable friend and influence. *When are you moving to Nashville?*

Colby Humphrey, Ben Crist, and Hugh Roberts: Thanks for being willing to read *part* of my first draft and helping me realize that a book that doesn't hold my friend's attention all the way through is obviously not ready to release to the world.

Shaun Tabatt & Jane Campbell: Thank you for being the first "industry" people to give me, and this book, the time of day. Your encouragement and feedback was value beyond appreciation.

Aaron Pierce and all of *Steiger International*: Thank you for giving *Come&Live!* and me a home. I'm inspired by your passionate commitment in reaching and discipling global youth culture for Jesus.

To the *Come&Live!* community past and present who graciously reminded me (and in many cases are still reminding me) that I'm not alone in the crazy: James Allen, Russ Hickman, Graham Howell, Nathan Mallon, Brad Davis, Andy Reale, Christie Craig, Corey Pigg, Joe Burgers, Jason Belcher, Maria Petty, Alex MacWilliams, Tom Rossmanith, Erin Brecht, Nyk Allen, Jeremy Davis, Ben Crist, Joshua Stump, Joey Elwood, Lukas Naugle, Michael Nusser, Dave Powers, Brian Harper and countless others who sacrificed time, energy, finances and comfort to help give a dream stronger legs. A grand portion of our early growth came through artists capturing the Father's heart in sincerity and generosity. *The Ember Days, Ascend The Hill, Preson Phillips, Showbread, Life In Your*

Way, White Collar Sideshow, Stevie Lujan, Great Awakening, Fallstar, Brian Campbell, Edge Kingsland, Sobre Todo Nombre, Daniel Bashta, Steve Schallert, DENS, Brian "Head" Welch, No Longer Music, Alegorica, Christafari, I Am Clay, The Walking Tree, Abel, Holding onto Hope, A Jesus Church, Bellarive, The Rock Music, Men As Trees Walking, Heroic Nation, Mike Steinkamp, Scruffhouse (are you guys healed of your Chadells yet?), *Crossfya, Artem Usov, Suitcase Sideshow, Jharmaine, Blien Vesne, SONS, Nuteki, Rivers & Robots, Mattie Montgomery* and *For Today, Levi The Poet, Sleeping Giant*: THANK YOU!

To the friend who I know will ask me why I forgot to include your name: You know who you are. Thank you!

About the Author.

Thirteen years ago, I was living in Seattle as a successful Christian music industry guy scrambling up a tall career ladder. But, I was also living in sin—hooked on drugs, pornography, pride, myself *and* work—struggling to love Jesus, let alone anyone else. Around the time my sin was at it's best, someone surprised me with a copy of *Don't Waste Your Life* by a passionate preacher named John Piper. That was about the time I realized that wasting my life was the one thing I was doing exceptionally well.

Early morning traffic was unusually frustrating on the Alaskan Way Viaduct while driving into *Tooth and Nail Record*'s posh Queen Anne office. All of us had come to a dead stop, inching forward so painfully that at one point I reached for my bag, pulled out my laptop, and tried getting wireless service off the elevated stretch of highway separating Elliott Bay from Seattle's emerald skyline. Right as I began thinking the only redeeming value for the absurd delay was the Olympic Mountain range showing off white peaks to my West, God met me.

I sensed Him speaking to me as quietly loud as I've ever heard His voice. He uttered just five words in the form of a question. "Why are you fighting Me?" broke through all my commuter and computer annoyance. I tried fighting back. "What do you mean, why am I fighting You?" came my own rhetorical verbal swing. I heard nothing in return, but what I felt right then, at age 30, has crucified my doubts and unbelief—landing me here, writing you this. It felt as though God had asked me the question that mattered most to my future, while simultaneously breaking off deep-seeded hardness of heart. Right there during the morning rush hour traffic jam with Mount Rainier in my rearview mirror—hoping none of my viaduct neighbors were noticing—I began crying, even awkwardly weeping, confessing my sin and asking Jesus to give me the kind of story He wanted to write most over my life.

In addition to avidly following Jesus, I'm a people lover, reader, husband, father, fan of quality coffee beans, Nashville-style Hot Chicken and creatively crafted ale. Beth, my wife of over twenty years, and our amazing kids, Sydney and David, share life with me in the rolling hills of West Nashville, TN.